SUMMARY

OF

CASTE

The Origins of Our Discontents by Isabel Wilkerson

LONNIE TRINIDAD

CONTENTS

PREFACE

All of the information, research, and anecdotes contained in this book belong to Isabel Wilkerson, the author of *Caste: The Origins of our Discontents*. This novel serves to streamline the narrative and theories presented by Wilkerson into more digestible knowledge for the average American. While none of the ideas are original, all are paraphrased from the research and multitude of stories that were used in constructing this powerful foundation for understanding the origin and perpetuation of caste in America. This novel explores the many facets of caste, concluding that it is caste and not racism or class that is the institutionalized system that prohibits the progress of racial equality in America. This book streamlines all the theories presented in the original book so that readers can maximize their time with the most relevant material from the text.

This book serves to educate the modern American on the invisible and pervasive caste system at work. As Wilkerson states, part of the pervasiveness of caste is, in part, due to its invisibility. As long as caste remains an invisible and undiscussed phenomenon within our economic, political and social systems then we will continue to collectively fail at ending it. It is only with its illumination that caste can be confronted and slowly dismantled. It is the goal of this book to ensure that everyone can access the education and narrative necessary to effectively rewrite the caste narrative that has been ascribed to our society at large. It also serves to propose brain science and humanity required to begin to face our bloodied past for a more amenable future.

In this book, you will learn how the creation of caste is completely arbitrary and entirely fabricated. You will learn about the perceptions and passed down beliefs from the colonists who came to this country and the African American slaves who built it. You will be able to see the ways in which caste was perpetuated in the United States and reinforced by countries like India and Germany who have both participated in a caste system. One of the most interesting conclusions drawn is the ways in which we can begin to reverse these generations of conditioning through mindfulness and compassion, all the way down to a cellular level. You will leave with the ability to scrutinize the larger caste system at work in addition to being able to see in which ways you perpetuate caste in your own life, with the hopes that all those who read this book will work to dismantle it.

PART 1 Toxins in the Permafrost and Heat Rising All Around

CHAPTER 1: The Afterlife of Pathogens Summary

The book, Caste, opens with a very grim scene. Wilkerson discusses the world caste system as something that had been laid dormant in our society for quite some time and compared our fragile society to a Siberian village. Due to global warming, the summer of 2016 in Siberia was extremely hot with temperatures reaching 95 degrees Fahrenheit. Parts of the landscape that had once been locked in ice became exposed to the air and the elements which led to anthrax poisoning. Anthrax had become encapsulated in dead reindeer carcasses that littered the landscape. Unbeknownst to the people who lived there, they had slowly become infected with the deadly disease due to the uncharacteristic rises in temperature. The caste system in the United States can be viewed with the same lens; the caste system may have been a dormant part of society but due to the increase in temperature, a pathogen has been released into the world and threatens to poison us all.

Wilkerson then turns her focus on the United States, a global superpower that influences everything from trade, economics, and technology during a pivotal moment; the 2016 election. Wilkerson goes into great depth in discussing the election and all of the heat that it brought with it, turning up the political, social, environmental, and economic dial all the way up until tensions have started boiling over. The 2016 election began with an "impetuous billionaire" for the conservative party and an overqualified woman for the liberal party. The man, transparently unqualified for the position of president, took to things like; boasting about sexually assaulting women and grabbing them by the vagina. He has since been named in more than 20 sexual misconduct allegations. He openly and publicly mocked a person with disabilities. He spread lies and false information about his competition and had supporters chanting things like, 'lock her up' at his presidential rallies. Wilkerson believes that these candidates divided a nation and the conservative candidate was seen to be upholding the old social order that benefits and appeals to white voters and, specifically, white men. White people of European dissent have been in the ruling class majority since the beginning of time and have always made up the dominant racial caste, according to Wilkerson. However, the white share of the population has been shrinking and it is reported in the text that by the year 2042, whites will no longer be the majority race in the United States.

Wilkerson looks at why and how these changes have taken place. While many people feel like this is a new wave of racism, Wilkerson argues that it is old racism and classism that had been frozen or embedded into society but with the political heat turned up, it has melted to the surface once again, infecting those who get too close to the source of the outbreak. The 2016 election was monumental for the world. The USA has seen 5 elections in which the electoral college has overruled the popular vote in order to decide the presidency. 2 of those cases have happened in the 21st century alone and 1 of those cases was the 2016 election. This election set the USA on a course of isolationism, tribalism, and the 'walling in' and protection of one's own, worship of wealth & acquisition at the expense of others and the planet as a whole. The biggest change however, was that the conservative candidate's election meant a change in social order. Confederate flags resurrected on the backs of cars and flown in front of homes signaling to neighbors and communities that these people desire to enslave other human beings. A resurgence of people who want others to 'know their place' in society and the world. The people who voted conservative felt like the country was finally moving toward aligning with a class system that people were born into like; having 'good genes', Trump's belief in the 'racehorse theory' of good blood, and the hierarchy of the ancestors.

A jump in hate crimes is just a small start at the shocking changes that accompanied the Trump presidency. Trump also took the US out of the Paris agreement that was meant to help the world slow down global warming and create more sustainable energy. Having sustainable energy and to control global warming means caring more about the longevity of our world and humanity over the short-term profit margins of big corporations. Trump continued by rolling back protections on air, water, national parks, and endangered species. Psychiatrists and psychologists from the top ivy-league universities began warning the American people of the dangerous, narcissistic man who now led the nation. These people tried to warn and protect us against the man who some called a danger to democracy and our government as we knew it. Trump began putting immigrant children behind bars, separating them from their parents and leaving many families apart to this very day. President Trump was described as an agent of a foreign power, with many cabinet members and advisors receiving and facing possible prison terms due to widening investigations into corruption. Trump was the 3rd president to ever go through an impeachment trial. Although he was impeached in the house, he was acquitted in the senate showing the single mindedness of the president and the president's followers who comprised the system of checks and balances that were thought to be built into the foundation of democracy. These changes led many to believe that the US no longer held a fully functional democracy. Wilkerson then discussed the impact that the coronavirus had on the American climate. President Trump informed the public that covid-19 was a Chinese virus that would disappear like a miracle. The president downplayed the severity of the virus and showed zero leadership and accountability in controlling it. Trump called the disease a 'hoax' first and then took to disparage those who disagreed with him or sought to forewarn him. As a result, the pandemic was the worst pandemic in recent history.

So, what created this rise in heat that let a poison back into the world of which we thought was slowly being eradicated? Wilkerson looks at the fabric of America and poses similar questions. This could have happened because coal miners and auto workers have become restless in a stagnant economy. This could have happened because people in America's heartland wanted to lash out at the country's coastal elites. This could have happened because the democratic candidate ran a floundering campaign or because minority voters didn't turn out to the polls in 2016. Wilkerson acknowledges that all of these things may be true. Yet it is still hard for so many liberal Americas to understand how the people who need healthcare, education, fair wages, and clean drinking water vote against their own interests.

Let's go back to the Siberian village with it's anthrax outbreak. The government was able to contain and eradicate the deadly outbreak by incinerating the 2,000 dead deer that were infected with the disease in combustion fields that reached up to 9500 degrees Celsius. The government doused the surrounding areas in bleach to curb the spread. People and reindeer were given vaccinations to protect them against the possibility of future infections.

The rising heat in the earth's oceans and the human heart could revive long buried threats. That some pathogens can never be killed, only contained. Only managed with vaccines against their expected mutations. An ancient and hearty virus required knowledge of its ever-present danger, caution to protect against exposure, and alertness to the power of its longevity; it's power to mutate, survive, and hibernate until it's reawakened. These contagions cannot be destroyed, not yet anyways, only managed and anticipated. Foresight and intelligence were the most effective antidote for now. Many of these phenomenons occur quietly and without damage until they are brought to the surface of the world and circumstances force us to search for the unseen stirrings of the human heart; to discover the origins of our discontents.

The Vitals of our History

Doctors wouldn't treat us without knowing our medical history and the medical history of our ancestors. We tell the doctor our symptoms, everything we have been exposed to, and everything we have survived. At the doctors, it doesn't serve us to minimize or ignore these things because they cannot be treated or our health understood when we ignore these factors. Looking at the history of our country can be akin to understanding that depression runs in our family or we are at a higher risk to develop breast cancer. We don't feel guilty or shameful in having these conversations. Instead, we educate ourselves about our lineage. We talk to specialists who can help us understand what we are facing. We find community to help us through the trials and tribulations of illness or disease. Ultimately, we try to learn how to fix it and we then pass down everything that we have learned and gained to the next generations so that they can protect themselves from harm. Wilkerson explains that when it comes to dealing with the illness of racism or our current day castes, we need to be willing to dive into our histories unapologetically in order for real healing to take place and to heal us ensure that our future generations do not suffer as we have.

CHAPTER 2: An Old House and an Infrared Light

Old houses can be amazing. They have history and character but they typically come with a host of problems. New owners of an old house may patch up cracks and holes when they move in. Yes, many issues that arise with an old house are unseen to the eye. It starts with a discolored wall or an unusual stain. Using a beam of light, professionals are able to better see the underlying symptoms of a larger internal issue. Wilkerson compares America to an old house that we have all inherited. The work on the house is never really complete. Natural disasters fight against a battered internal structure whose flaws were left untended to by the previous inhabitants. When a storm hits, you may not go into the basement because you don't want to see the damage that was caused by the storm. We are choosing not to look at our own peril because the foundational issues that we are ignoring will not go away. Ignorance is not protection from the consequences of inaction.

We have all inherited a piece of land that is stunning on the outside but whose foundation is built on rocks and sand. The foundation is left heaving and contracting over generations of inaction. Small issues have been patched up over the decades but the larger issues remain. People who have inherited such a property may rightly say that they are not to be blamed for the condition of the house when they were gifted it. They didn't have any say to the foundation on which the house was built, which is true. But that does not absolve us of our responsibility to fix the structural issues that persist in our newly acquired home. It is our duty to tend to the deeper problems before passing the home off to the next generation.

Mold and toxins only get worse, spreading and mutating over time before they infect everyone in the house and those outside of it. Instead of treating the mold we put buckets under leaky ceilings and we carefully step over rotting floorboards. We adjust to the house and these issues become more acceptable to us. The awkwardness of living this way becomes acceptable. The acceptable becomes convenient and, if we live long enough, the unthinkable becomes normal. Yet, just like in a house, we cannot fix the problems that exist unless we can see it. We need to remove the plaster and wallpaper that have been slapped over unsightly problem after unsightly problem. We need to get down to the bones of the house which Wilkerson presents at the caste system. The caste system is the unseen skeleton of America that was built long ago. Caste is the infrastructure of our divisions that design social order and, yet, it is also an artificial construction. It is a fixed and embedded ranking system of human value that pits the presumed inferiority of a group passed on ancestry and immutable traits. Traits that, on their own, do not hold meaning are assigned meaning within the caste system that favors the dominant caste since they are the ones who designed it.

There are three notable caste systems that Wilkerson discusses in this chapter which are; the caste system of Nazi Germany, the lingering caste system of India, and the race-based caste pyramid in the United States. Each version is based on stigmatizing those deemed inferior to justify the dehumanization that is necessary to keep the lowest ranked people at the bottom and to rationalize the protocols of enforcing the caste.

This means that even people who fall somewhere in between the highest caste and the lowest don't question the system and go along with the will of those in the upper caste. The caste systems are typically founded and reinforced through sacred texts or the laws of nature which are justified throughout the culture and passed down through generations. Caste is ultimately about the distribution of power; which groups have it and which do not. It's about resources. Caste is an explicit way for people in power to decide who is worthy of resources and who is not in addition to who gets to acquire and control the resources that are available. Caste is about deciding who is worthy of things like respect, authority, and assumption of competence and who are not afforded such things. Caste is the unseen guide that exists beyond our awareness that forces us to rank human characteristics. All of the three caste systems have these traits in common but the caste system in the United States is detrimental because it is the one that has gone unseen and untended to for so many centuries that is has become an engrained piece of our human psyche and we have normalized stereotypes that have been used to justify brutalities against entire groups in our species.

The caste system in America is based on race. This means that our basis of humans is based entirely upon appearance and race serves as a tool and visible decoy for caste. Race is a means of dividing humans by assigning assumptions and values to physical features. This way of thinking has become ingrained in our subconscious and race serves as a visual cue for humans to assign assumptions about others. Race becomes the determining factor about:

- How a person should be treated

- Where they are expected to live

- What kinds of positions they are expected to hold

- Whether they belong in a certain neighborhood or board room

- Whether or not we allow them to speak with authority on a subject

- Whether or not we allow them to receive pain medication at the hospital

- Whether their neighborhood is likely to be situated next to a toxic waste site

- Whether they will die during childbirth

- Whether they will be shot by the people in power meant to protect them

In the history of the United States, race was always used to divide people into extreme groups. The ones who created the caste system attached meaning to these extremes only to reinforce those meanings by recreating them into roles that each caste is assigned, permitted, or required to perform. Caste and race are not synonymous or mutually exclusive but rather, co-exist and reinforce one another. In America, race is the visible agent of the unseen force of caste. If caste is, indeed, the bones than race is the skin. Race is the physical traits that we can see and, alone, they have no real meaning. Despite the inherent lack of meaning in race, it has become shorthand for who a person is and caste is the powerful infrastructure that holds each group in its place.

Wilkerson moves on to let readers know that caste is fixed while race is fluid and superficial. Race is subjected to constant redefinition in order to meet the needs of the dominant caste. Race is an entirely made up construct by humans and is always being adjusted in order to fit the narrative of the majority. Requirements to qualify as white have changed depending on the needs of the dominant caste and whoever fit the definition of white in whatever point in history was granted the rights and privileges of the dominant caste. On the other side of the spectrum, the subordinate caste has been fixed from the beginning. This resulted in generations being born into a silent war game listed in teams that were not of our own choosing. We were assigned teams by the race uniform that we all wear. The uniform that signals our growth and potential to others. The use of inherited characteristics in order to differentiate ability and group value is the way that culture has been used to create and maintain a caste system. Wilkerson notes that assigning a person to a caste according to physical traits surpasses all other categories, even gender, in intensity and subordination.

CHAPTER 3: An American Untouchable

The chapter opens when Wilkerson paints a picture of 1959, when Martin Luther King Jr. and his wife traveled to visit India, specifically the old city of Bombay, to visit Gandhi, the father of peaceful protests. King was interested in seeing the place and speaking with the leaders who fought against British rule and to see the caste system in India first hand. Despite claiming independence from British rule, the India social system still recognized an old caste system and King was interested in learning about the "untouchable" who are the lowest caste in India and have very much been left behind as the rest of the country evolves. Martin Luther King visited a high school in a city that houses all of the untouchables and, thus, the children that attended the school were untouchables themselves. When King was introduced to the students, their teacher introduced Martin Luther King Jr. as an American untouchable. For a moment, King was rather insulted by the idea. He had just flown in a place halfway across the world. He had just dined with the country's Prime Minister. He had been giving out autographs in the airport and while touring the city. Upon pondering the sentiment deeper, King realized that Black people in America have been fighting for equal rights for centuries but were still battling poverty, subjected to the ghettos and exiled in their own country much like the untouchables of India. King realized in that moment that he was an untouchable, that all black people in America were, indeed, untouchables as well. King's epiphany meant that he acknowledged the caste system in the United States for the first time. He noticed that he had been a part of this caste system his whole life and this system laid beneath all the forces he was fighting against in America.

More than a century and a half before the American revolution, a human hierarchy evolved in the United States with the concept of "birthright". Birthright extends from the idea of entitled expansion that brought the world's first democracy in addition to a ranking of human value and usage. Christopher Columbus didn't discover America, rather, America was already home to many indigenous people and tribes. Upon European settlement in America, greed and self-reverence eclipsed the consciousness of men, resulting in invaders taking land and human bodies at their will. The invaders looked to civilize the wilderness of America to their liking by conquering and then either enslaving or removing the people who already lived on the land. The indigenous people were deemed to be lesser beings than the European and the settlers extracted all the wealth they could from the earth and shorelines. To justify these atrocities, European settlers adopted the belief that their way was right and every other way was wrong. Settlers turned to their own self-interested interpretation of the bible in order to create a hierarchy of who could do what, who could own what, and who was on top versus who was on bottom in addition to who was in between. In this ranking system, there emerged a ladder of humanity.

Invaders came to the lands out west with guns and resources that far outweighed the fire power of the indigenous people. Invaders won the battle over land and these invaders were ranked in descending order by their proximity to those who were in power. The ranking continued downward until we arrived at the very bottom, African captives who were transported to the western world to build it and serve the victors for the rest of their days and through generations. In this foundation, there developed a caste system based on what people looked like that remained unspoken and unnamed by citizens. People began acting upon it unconsciously and still do to this day. Just like the studs and beams give a building infrastructure, caste gave the United States it's infrastructure. Its invisibility is what gives it power and longevity. Though it comes in and out of consciousness and flares itself during times of upheaval, there is an ever present through line in the way America operates to this day.

Caste became an idea that was used during the antebellum abolitionist fighting segregation in public schools. The nature of a current-day caste became a violation of equality. Ultimately, we cannot understand the current upheavals without accounting for the human pyramid that exists subconsciously within us all. Just as the DNA is a code for cell development, caste is the operating system for all economic, political, and social development in the USA. America created the caste system as a way to maintain the color line which has been a way of keeping people of color in their place. As discussed earlier, race is a human invention not a biological construct. To understand the disparities in the United States it is imperative that we look at the caste system of America which is more central to the heart of disparities that people in America face.

Caste filters down to every branch of life, setting the expectations of where we fit on the ladder. The racial creed of the south said something akin to, let the lowest white man count for more than the highest negro.

This meant that Irish indentured servants were given more autonomy and respect than black servants and white servants still believed in white supremacy. Caste is unavoidable and follows people everywhere. It is important to understand the way in which caste works to benefit those in power and systemically hurt those who are not in the dominant caste. To understand America, it's imperative that we look at the hidden work of a caste system that had gone unnamed for centuries and yet prevails among us to our collective detriment. We must open our eyes to see all that we have in common with one another and with other cultures we might otherwise dismiss. To summon the courage of understanding and to listen to one another will bring us the answers that we so desperately search for. At the end of the day, racism does not define America's culture; however, caste certainly does.

An Invisible Program

There is a small portion of the population that believe life is like a computer simulation. This theory of reality believes that humans are programs and that the external world and our program mesh to form our individual perspectives. Humans who don't question their programming can lead happy but ignorant lives as captives to the simulation. People who don't know they are captive will not upset their reality by questioning things around them. Those who do realize that they are captives to a simulation or program may try to fight our programming to find that the programming fights back. We are all governed by programming that mostly goes unnoticed, deeply embedded into the drone of existence, these programs are invisible just like the caste system is. Caste in the guise or normalcy (ie. Injustices looking just, atrocities looking unavoidable) keep the machinery humming in order to maintain the privacy of those hoarding and holding tight to power.

PART 2 The Arbitrary Construction of Human Divisions

CHAPTER 4: A Long-Running Play and the Emergence of Caste in America

Wilkerson opens this chapter by exploring the parallels between the cast of a play and acting as part of a caste system in America. People are given roles to play, their costumes handed out at birth can be neither changed nor removed. The cast grows accustomed to who plays each part and if you stay in the roles long enough, actors begin to believe that these roles are preordained. The cast becomes associated with the characters that they play, public opinion deciding day in and out who is good and who is bad. Veering from the script or speaking out of character will get you demoted or replaced. The overarching idea is that when we're playing a part in a play, we're not really being ourselves or expressing who we are as people. Wilkerson sees that we are all players on a stage that was built even long before our ancestors arrived on Western land.

Late in 1619, a year before the pilgrims made it to Plymouth Rock, a man named John Rolfe made it to Virginia. Captured slaves from a Spanish ship were sold to the British and ended up being brought over to the Western world for enslavement. What the colonizers originally had planned for these captured enslaved, we cannot be sure. It could have been a short-term indentured servitude or they could have sent the slaves over expecting them to be enslaved for a lifetime but we will never know their original intentions.

A hierarchy began to form in 1630 due to a rough attempt at a colonial census. Few Africans were seen as important enough to have their names listed on the census report by name and often excluded all other details about them like; when they arrived, and age. This information was vital in establishing the terms and time frames of indentured servitude. European indentured servants; however, were accurately accounted for on the census, proving that from the very beginning, African servants were not seen as equal to their white counterparts.

Before the caste system developed in the USA as we now know it, there was the colonial caste system in Virginia. Caste is a completely arbitrary construction that is meant to change and be fluid enough to fit the needs of the dominant caste for them to maintain control and power. Thus, the caste system began on the basis of religion. Yes, in the beginning it was religion and not race that defined the status of people in the original colonies. The dominant caste was Christian and practicing Christianity meant that European workers would be mostly exempt from lifetime enslavement. This also meant that indigenous people were condemned, followed closely by Africans because neither observed

Christianity, which the settlers decided was the hallmark of a civilized society. This began the process of testing the bounds of human categories whenever the colonists had a decision to make.

After a while, African slaves began to convert to Christianity which posed a challenge to the religion-based hierarchy that the colonists tried to establish. African efforts to fully participate in the colonies were met with stark resistance by colonists who were hungry for the cheapest and most compliant labor possible in order to extract the most wealth from the Western world. As slaves worked tirelessly on tobacco, cotton, and rice farms they made the crops thrive. White farmers had not worked in such conditions before and were unfamiliar with growing these crops. It quickly became evident to the white farm owners that without African labor, their enterprises would surely fail. European indentured servants were easily able to run away from their owners and blend into another caste. Africans, on the other hand, were not afforded the same luxury because no person from a different caste looked like he did. This resulted in colonizers trying to replace all European indentured servants with African ones, so that slaves could no longer run off and escape their fates. This hardened the population into a single caste system of which Africans were at the bottom.

In the 1600's Africans were not just slaves but hostages that were subjected to unspeakable tortures that their captors documented without remorse. No one was ever willing to pay a ransom for their rescue. Our country doesn't like to talk about slavery because America is seen as a shining beacon of democracy. Slavery is commonly dismissed as only a sad chapter in the countries young history and is quick to be brushed under the rug. Yet, you cannot heal something by ignoring it. The same way you can't heal trauma like domestic violence you experienced as a child or alcoholism that runs in your family. The country cannot heal until we confront the basis of our economic and social order for more than a quarter of a millennium. Slavery was not an unfortunate thing that happened to black people, but was an American innovation and institution that was created for the elites and the dominant caste and enforced by the poorer members of the dominant caste who tied their lot to the caste system rather than their conscious.

Slavery from 1619-1865 was marked by legally sanctioned violence with a web of enforcers. American slavery meant that victims were punished as a lesson to others. This extreme form of slavery didn't exist anywhere else in the world and left an entire category of the human race ruled out and forced to remain an unsightly subgroup that was to remain enslaved for generations because they were not seen as even being human. The American institution of slavery meant that slaves:

- Were worked as long as the owners desired
- Have no rights over their bodies or their loved ones (children)
- Could be mortgaged
- Could be bet or gambled
- Could be bred
- Could be given as wedding presents
- Could be sold to spouses or children
- Could be used to settle an estate
- Regularly whipped or branded
- Regularly raped

- Subjected to any whim of the people who owned them
- Castration

Before the United States of America existed as we know it, there was slavery. A living debt passed down for 12 generations. Slaves were at the entire will of their masters. They were beaten, whipped, and starved simply because masters wished it to be so. Farmers whipped the slaves who underperformed and they whipped the ones who exceeded even harder. Whipping severed as a gateway form of violence that led to bizarre sadism as slavery unfolded in America. Every means of torture like waterboarding and mutilation. Southerns typically minimized the horrors which they inflicted and had grown accustomed to. Slavers weren't allowed to raise a hand in defense, weren't allowed to stick up for themselves or for their enslaved peers. They had no protection under the law and were never compensated for their long hours of work. They have fewer protections than the cattle in the fields. Slaves worked up to 15 hours per day and subsisted on a mere piece of corn per week that they needed to mill by hand at night, after they completed their 15 hours in the fields. Owners sometimes only allowed meat for protein once per year. Enslavers were the wealthiest people in the world due to having slaves and their profits from their farms soared.

The majority of African American slaves lived in complete terror of their owners for 246 years in the United States. This was due to the fact that no slave owners ever faced any time of punishment or sanction for the atrocities that they would commit. During this time of slavery, white people became used to regulating negro insubordination by force and with the consent of law enforcement. Slavery perverted the balance of power so that it made the degradation of the subordinate caste normal and righteous. Plantations became hugely popular in the south and were essentially prisoner camps whose prisoners committed the crime of having dark skin. This was the way of life in America for much longer than it was not. It took the Civil War, the deaths of over half a million soldiers and civilians, the assassination of Abe Lincoln, and the passage of the 13th amendment to bring the institution of slavery to an end.

For 12 years after the Civil War, a time known as the Reconstruction, the north sought to rebuild the south by helping 4 million newly liberated slaves leave their plantations. But the federal government withdrew from the south for political expediency and left those in the subordinate caste in the unregulated hands of the people who had enslaved them for generations. The dominant caste quickly got to work devising a labyrinth of laws that held the newly freed people on the bottom rung even more tightly. People could be beaten or killed with impunity for any breach of the caste system, like not stepping off the sidewalk quickly enough or trying to vote. The dominant caste controlled everything and they created the caste system that worked to reinforce itself. They designated the lowest caste as dumb because they were not legally allowed to be taught to read or write. They were depicted as lazy to justify the bull whip. Slaves were said to be immoral which justified their rape and forced breeding. Slaves were depicted as criminals because the colonists made the response of defending themselves or trying to break free from their prison's the conditions of a crime.

The caste system pits the extremes in human pigmentation at the opposite ends. As immigration began, people came to America from Europe through Ellis Island. They were forced to shed their old selves in order to adapt to this new land, many of them trying to figure out how to position themselves in the hierarchy. Many people needed to drop their nationalities of Polish, Czech, Hungarian, etc. in order to become white. White became a political designation that only has meaning when set against something that is not white. Groups who had warred against each other for years were fused together in order to fit into the dominant caste in America. These people did not have the same faith, values, or beliefs but were connected by the color of their skin. The European immigrants' experience was shaped by whiteness. It was the most important possession that one could lay claim to and it was their whiteness that opened the golden door. This only served to strengthen the dominant caste in the hierarchy.

Immigrants who wanted to belong to the dominant caste needed to prove themselves as white which meant defining themselves as not black. It was important that they learn how to be white. They observed the way that black people were treated and imitated or one-upped the disdain and content that the dominant caste members showed black people. They learned racial epithets and even joined in on violence against blacks in order to gain admittance to the dominant caste. Once they proved themselves as part of the dominant caste they were afforded all the opportunity they could dream of. It wasn't that the white immigrant groups economic successes came at the expense of non-whites, but that they owe their now stabilized and broadly recognized whiteness itself, in part, to those non-white groups.

The institution of slavery distorted human relationships. Instead of compassion, empathy, and curiosity about other people's way of life, colonizers put people into groups based on an arbitrary trait. One side was made to perform the role of subservience. They were forced to curb innate talents and suppress emotions like; pain, anger, frustration, and grief. On the other side, the dominant caste lived under the illusion of innate superiority over all other groups of humans. They told themselves that the slaves they kept as property and worked for 18 hours a day without pay were not people but beasts of the field. In the act of dehumanizing Africans, the dominant caste also dehumanized themselves. Americans today have inherited these distorted rules of engagement whether or not their families had enslaved people or have even been in the country at that time. Slavery would become the social, economic, and psychological template that shaped our nation for generations.

CHAPTER 5: "The Container We Have Built for You"

The most important yet unspoken rule of caste is that the lowest caste was to remain low in every way, at all times, and at any cost. The dominant caste always looked for ways to reinforce the lower castes inferiority. Black men were not to be addressed as Mister and black women were never to be addressed as Miss or Missus. Instead they were called by their first name, auntie, or gal no matter their age or marital status.

In Birmingham a white supremist police chief rigged a local election by framing the man whom he wanted to lose. His plan was to pay a black man to shake the hand of the man he wanted to frame at the same time a photographer happened to be walking by to snap a picture. The next day, a full-page article was published in the newspaper, thanks to the police chief, and it destroyed the man's campaign. At the time, it was a cardinal sin to shake a black man's hand in public and it cost him the election.

In the town of Selma, right outside of Birmingham, black people had become determined to vote. It was 1965, 100 years since the end of the Civil War that ended slavery and yet the subordinate caste will still not able to vote. It was in Selma that a young black boy was forced to call his mother and grandmother by their first names when out in public and he watched other people from the dominant caste do the same. He was furious at the lack of respect for his family and vowed that if he ever had a daughter, he would name her Miss. The boy was Harold Hale and when he grew up he did have a daughter who he would name Miss. Harold grew up and left Alabama in exchange for Texas.

Miss and her family were the only black family that lived on the block in their Texas neighborhood. Harold loved his yard and took impeccable care of it. He would change the flower arrangements every night so that when people woke in the morning, they would always see a new and exciting arrangement in the yard. Others had assumed that Harold was nothing more than hired help but once they knew that he was the owner, people beat his mailbox with a baseball bat. After the incident, Harold cemented in his mailbox and the next person who drove by the house with a bat hanging out the window broke their arm. People in the community left the mailbox alone after that.

Miss soon started at the local high school that had recently been integrated. In a time before cell phones the girls at the high school would use walkie talkies in order to meet up in between periods and before lunch. The principal noticed the students gathering around lockers and congregating in groups in the hallways during their break times. The principal was floored when he saw the groups in the halls and loitering outside lockers. He called Miss into his office and peppered her with questions about her activities at school and where she came from. She told him that they had moved there from Alabama and that her father worked for a Fortune 500 company, something her dad had taught her to say in order to deflect dominant caste members from acts of aggression. When he asked for her name, she obliged, telling him that her name was Miss. He grew annoyed, asking for her name again and again, each time she responded with her name. The principal, tired of this, asked his secretary to see her records. When he saw that her name was, in fact, Miss he let her go for the day. He was frustrated by the breech in caste that was forced upon him by Harold Hale and his refusal to abide by caste norms.

Wilkerson recounts a time when she worked for the NY Times as a reporter. She had flown to a city and was only there conducting interviews for the day. She had made it to her last appointment of the day and walked into the store to meet with the man whom she had made an appointment with. Isabel was told by an employee of the store that the man was expected to return shortly from another appointment. Isabel waited for a moment when a man entered the store in a frenzy. The employee indicated to Wilkerson that this was the man she had been waiting for. Isabel went to introduce herself but was quickly dismissed by the man saying that he was running late for an appointment and that he couldn't speak with her. Isabel insisted that she was his appointment but the man refused to believe her. He asked for identification which Isabel provided but the man would not meet with her because he refused to believe that the black women standing in front of him could be a NY Times reporter. She left and flew back home to publish the article without the man's interview.

Each of us is in a container sometimes. The label on the container signals to the world what might be inside the container and what to do with what is inside. The label might also give you other hints and clues like, what self the container belongs on. In a caste system, the label on the outside doesn't usually match the contents on the inside. This means that the container is typically put on the wrong shelf. This hurts people and institutions in ways that we may not even know.

CHAPTER 6: The Measure of Humanity

Height, like skin pigment, is fairly consistent within familial and tribal communities. Yet, it would be silly to justify lowly or elevated positions in a caste based on height. What if it were height, not skin color, that we used as a means of categorizing human beings? Height would be the determining factor that determines who is intelligent, beautiful, desirable, and wealthy. It is hard to imagine and seems laughable but the horrors inflicted on differences in skin color are not.

Race has been constructed by humans in order to create social distance and has no basis in biology. 1795 was the first time that the word Caucasian was used. An anthropologist who loved studying skulls began trying to classify them and their distinct characteristics. He named his favorite skull after the Caucus mountains in Germany, where the skull was found. The entire concept of race is man-made. No children playing together would identify one another using the political terms of white, black, or latinx. Americans clutch to race like we do to superstition. Racism didn't exist in the western culture until colonizers made it so.

What we're currently facing is an adjustment to the definition of racism that is constantly being adjusted. Social scientists define racism as one group having authority over another. Racism has come to mean a hatred of a certain group. Racism has become a term that people constantly deflect. Who, after all, could be racist in a country that proudly flies the confederate flag. Racism is not an either/or situation. It is easily deniable and impossible to measure. Racism has been found to fall on a continuum with people falling somewhere in between two extremes. Caste gives racism structure.

Caste is the granting or withholding of things like human kindness and respect. Caste isn't hatred or anger but it is the upholding of a hierarchy. Keeping those who are disfavored on the rung below you as a means of elevating oneself. Race and racism can sometimes detract from caste. A caste system is what holds everyone in a fixed place. The dominant caste is highly invested in keeping the hierarchy as it is. It is not the hate of a group but people of the dominant caste are not interested in changing it. People become categorized by stereotypes. When we feel a pang of shock and resentment when someone from a marginalized group steps out of their assigned place in society, that is the effect of caste. When the structure is breached, people become uneasy and upset. Caste is not an ancient relic that people can wish away. Its invisibility made it substantial and pervasive. We will never get over it until we realize how deep caste runs.

CHAPTER 7: Through the Fog of Delhi to the Parallels in India and America

Wilkerson recounts walking along a sidewalk in India seeing it adorned with colorful flowers, incense, and offers. As she strolled along the sidewalk that burst with color and the sweet smell of figs, she was reminded about the shrines and alters that adorn the streets here in America. Typically, they are erected to honor a loss but Wilkerson likes to imagine that Americans, like Indians, simply desire to connect with or honor something beyond ourselves. America and India now are vastly different but they used to be far more similar.

Both America and India are protected by great oceans, and ruled by Britain for a time. Both adopted social hierarchies that continue to shape the respective countries today. Those who were deemed the lowest in the land served those deemed the highest. The countries used the same instructional manual but translated it to fit their distinctive cultures. Kept the dominant caste above and separate from those deemed lower and both exiled their indigenous people to the outsides of society. They also both used terror and force to keep them there. America and India both abolished legal slavery but caste prevails in both lands due to the hearts and habits of the institutions and infrastructures that monitor it.

Both countries are marked by bonding people of lower caste to those in the dominant caste through debt. This manifested in Africans working endlessly to pick cotton or tobacco in order to pay off their own debt or generational debt. Dalits were forced to pick tea and suffer the same fate. While slavery is an antiquity from the past, both groups are still confined to their fixed roles in society to this day. Society is no longer allowed to discriminate against others based on their race, religion, or sex. Things like reservations and affirmative action have worked to make right a clearly unbalanced scale. Both of these measures created to combat the discrimination that typically accompanies racism and caste-ism and the measures are equally unpopular with the upper castes in both countries. There is this idea of reverse racism, when people in the dominant caste feel as though they are being denied opportunity that is rightfully theirs. Yet, no one person has cornered the market on opportunity or humanity.

America, who started as a two-tiered hierarchy, began to shift with immigration to the United States. The immigrants from Europe made up most of the middle caste which didn't seem to affect or bother the dominant caste much. In India, there is an elaborate thread work that splits people into 5 different castes. Caste originates from divinity in India's culture and divinity alone assigned people to their respective castes. Depending on what caste people are born into determines the kind of work that they will be permitted to do. Finally, people in India wear their caste with their name. People from all castes are used to being asked their surname and what village they are from in order to determine what caste they are a part of. In India, dominant caste people believe that their caste is the natural order and that the lowest caste embraces their position while colonists believed that Africans were better off enslaved than in their own country. What both cultures are missing; however, is the desire of all human beings to be free.

CHAPTER 8: The Nazis and the Acceleration of Caste

Nazi's had their own influence on the caste system. Their goal was to isolate Jewish people from Arian people. In 1894, Germany enacted the Nuremberg laws that were an attempt to protect society from the disfavor of the Jews. When Nazi's began their rise to power, it was America that they turned to in order to see what could be learned from the people there. The Nazis specifically wanted to know how the United States was able to marginalize specific groups while upholding and guarding white citizenry. Hitler attributed the success of America to their Arian aptitude and wanted Germany to follow suit.

Hitler was highly interested in the way in which America used the law to solidify racial impurity. He watched how the country governed interracial marriage and education and wanted to enact something similar for themselves in Germany. Additionally, Nazis looked at their own legal system compared to Americas. All of the cases that had been brought to the Supreme Court on accounts of racial injustice sided on the dominant caste's side. The Nazis found this encouraging as they had court cases much like those in America and felt confident that they would be victorious as those in America were. Nazis were amazed at the American lynching process and were specifically impressed that the dominant caste was able to maintain innocence while murdering thousands of people in the subordinate caste.

Hitler was originally picked to go into politics to be a puppet. He was supposed to do what he was told but he was a much more opinionated and charismatic leader than anyone originally gave him credit for. Hitler reigned for 12 years and his goal was to destroy and exploit democracy. He became a cult figure, a chosen savior anointed by God. Nazis began to close in on the Jews, donning Sanskrit symbols that we now know as the Nazi swastika. Jews were blamed as scapegoats for the monetary fallout from the war that Germany just lost in addition to the loss itself. They restricted Jews from dominant caste positions like doctors, businessmen, or judges. They restricted Jews from dominant caste positions like doctors, businessmen, or judges. Nazis began to police the amount of land that Jews had and they were slowly closing in on them; tightening the noose metaphorically and, in some cases, literally.

America went to such great lengths to segregate whites from blacks that the colonists were able to make it look like a normal part of society. Because race is politically constructed, almost every state in America had a different definition for what made a person black. Hitler looked to the Americans for how to treat ambiguous-looking people in Germany. He decided that the person would go to the disfavored group if they were known to fraternize with the disfavored caste. Anyone that was Jewish or half Jewish were cut off from their Arian family members and people began to turn one another into the Gestapo. This was taken from the Association Clause that the colonists had created in America, specifically, Texas and North Carolina, used this clause to determine whether or not someone belonged to the lower caste. In Germany, a person would be defined by the Nuremberg Laws as a Jew if they had 3 or more Jewish grandparents. A person didn't even need to be Jewish in order to fit the criteria under this context. Many Germans who had not practiced Judaism for many years were caught in the grip of Nazi terror. While this definition of Jews was harsh, it is nothing compared to the unforgiving hardness of the one drop rule in America. This rule stated that if a person had even one drop of African blood in them, they were considered black. The one drop rule was even too harsh for the Nazi's to adopt proving that American laws were the foundation of the most racist regime in the modern world.

CHAPTER 9: The Evil of Silence

Evil has a way of growing, spreading, and mutating. This particular evil had grown too big for just one person to stop it. The evil rained down from the sky, landing on their gingerbread cottages. The people that lived there simply went to sweep up the ash wordlessly. As they did so, trying to ignore the rows of empty homes that once belonged to the people whose ashes they were sweeping. Those who remain silent in the face of evil are complicit to it. While many people that lived in Germany were not Nazis, most of them were complicit with Nazi lies. The lies that Nazis spread about Jews and homosexuals were not human like themselves but, subhuman.

In America, a large Sycamore tree was planted in a most inconvenient spot. It disrupted traffic, it caused accidents, and it was mostly a burden. Despite these issues with the tree, the townspeople insisted on keeping it. Not because it was a lovely tree, but because of what the large tree symbolized; the lynching of black people. One day, over 500 people gathered around that tree to watch a boy burn to death. Wylie McNeely was wrongly targeted during a citizen's arrest that turned into a kidnapping. A little girl was allegedly attacked while walking home from Sunday school. The girl made no mention of Wylie but a group of men in the town saw him at the corner store and believed him to be the culprit. No trial, no goodbyes to his loved ones, no real explanation as to why this was happening to him. While the boy was burning alive, the men debated over which body parts would be kept by who.

Lynching's in America were an event that was part carnival and part horror show. As technology improved with the times, photographers would be notified about when lynchings would be taking place and they would show up to the site of the lynching and take photographs for people. They would bring printing presses to the lynchings and would print out images for people right there on the spot. People loved attending the lynchings and would often get their photographs framed or they would send them as a postcard to relatives. Lynching postcards soon became a cornerstone of the postcard industry. Even Nazis in Germany would never be so bold or stoop so low as to take pictures or hold tours of the horrors that went on at the concentration camps. In America though, torturing and humiliating black people was a regular occurrence. The images that were being sent back and forth to loved ones became so grossly sickening to the mail workers that they tried to have the lynching postcards banned. Yet, in truly American fashion, we decided to put them in envelopes and send them that way instead.

PART 3 The Pillars of Caste

The Foundations of Caste: The Origins of Our Discontents

After studying three of the most prolific caste systems of the world, commonalities among the castes began to take shape. In order to create such an impressionable and long-lasting system, there must be unseen pillars that work to uphold the belief system. There are 8 pillars that have been identified as necessary to creating and maintaining a caste system.

1.   DIVINE WILL AND THE LAWS OF NATURE

The Indians have a divine tale that discusses the caste system and everyone's role within it. India's entire caste system is based on the idea that the caste in which a person is born is a divine right. In India caste can best be understood by looking at the body. There are the feet and legs which are the foundational caste of farmers and laborers. The middle caste includes the core which represents merchants and businessmen. The arms represent warriors and soldiers. The final caste is the head and that represents the shamans and healers. There is also one caste that is not a part of the body at all, the lowest caste is merely the shadow in this analogy; tied to the body wherever it may go but never really a part of it. They are the Dalits also known as the Untouchables and they are the most subordinate caste in India. Divine will and the laws of nature are inherent in any caste system.

2.   INHERITABILITY

In the United States, children inherited the caste that their mother belonged to. This was not always the case, for in Europe children take on the caste of their fathers traditionally. This change was calculated on the part of the colonists who were now able to turn the black womb into a gold mine for slave owners. Slave owners were able to have sex with their slaves and even impregnate them. Once they gave birth, the children would stay in the slave quarters with their mother only to be enslaved by their father as well. Many slave owners would sell their own children and black women became all the more profitable to them. Membership to the lowest caste seemed immutable and inescapable for children born into slavery couldn't marry or work his way out of it. It is the fixed nature of caste that makes it so hard to escape. Many people seem to mistake class for caste but they are very different. Class can be acquired through hard work and ingenuity. You can learn and acquire class. There is nothing that you can earn or lose in order to be in the lowest caste. If you can act your way out of it, it is not caste but class.

The Hindu caste system has provided a similar hierarchy to that of the caste system in America. In India, caste decides the trajectory of a person's life from birth. Not wealth or celebrity will help people who are identified as belonging to the subordinate caste. Professional athletes from all over the country have been harassed by people in the dominant caste for no visible reason. One black basketball player had his leg broken and a football player was choked out by a police officer when he tried to help break up a fight. These professional athletes have status and wealth on their side but when they are out in the community are still only seen as a black person and they are punished for it.

3.   ENDOGAMY

Endogamy is the restricting of marriage to one's own caste. This was brutally enforced by the United States by prohibiting romantic interest and sexual partnership with people from opposing castes. Endogamy is ordained by God which makes prohibiting love between humans acceptable in a caste system. The goal is to have the dominant caste look down so much on the subordinate caste that they are no longer seen as human and that the subordinate caste needed to be regulated at all times.

A white man of the middle caste was sentenced to a whipping for having sexual relations with a black woman. It wasn't just a whipping though, but a public flogging. This meant that the white man was being punished so that he might not have relations with a black person again. He was cast out of the dominant group and was now able to be punished. This served as a warning to other white people that they would also be punished for the transgression. A lot of white southern slave owners were not happy about this rule but the continued to rape their slaves anyways. In these situations, the women were punished for seducing the men. They would even be whipped while pregnant with their owner's child. Some states even outlawed marriages between white people and the indigenous people and Asians punishable with fines and prison time. Upper caste men who wrote the laws fixed their lot so that they also wouldn't need to answer to them. They controlled who had access to whom and it served to further reinforce the caste system along with the message that white men had all the power.

4.   PURITY

The obsession with purity can be seen in all the three major caste systems that have been covered in this book. Purity is a way in which the upper caste is able to protect its sanctity over the lower caste. The Untouchables in India needed to remain 12 to 96 steps away from those in the dominant caste so as not to pollute them with even their shadow. Untouchables are forced to wear a bell so that other people can become aware of their presence and leave before they are tainted and if they did come into contact with a Dalit, they needed to undergo ritual purification in order to cleanse themselves.

In the United States, the subordinate caste studied from different textbooks. Black people had to drink water from horse tropes while whites had their own fountains. Black people were not permitted to try on clothes while shopping and sometimes they weren't even allowed into stores at all. Black people had separate cemeteries, ambulances, hospital wings, and train platforms. America had created a separate but equal philosophy that they boasted but nothing was equal about the upper and lower castes living conditions. There was a lower caste man who worked on a railroad. While working on the job he was injured and a group of onlookers called an ambulance, trying to save his life. When the ambulance pulled up and saw that the man was black, they turned around and left him there to die.

Black people were banned from white beaches, pools, and lakes. White people went to great lengths to enforce this. People in the dominant caste began throwing glass and nails into public pools so that no one could use them. A 17-year-old boy, Eugene Williams, swam past an imaginary line while playing around in the lake and he was stoned and drowned to death for the transgression. Black people were held under water, drowning in public pools. If a black person entered a pool, white people insisted that the pool be drained, scrubbed, and refilled with fresh water before they would use it again.

Policing of purity meant that the United States needed to define what it meant to be in the dominant caste. The colonists decided that even one single drop of African, Asian, or Indigenous blood would mean that someone was impure. This ultimately became white supremacy, granting honorary whiteness to those who looked close enough to those in the dominant caste.

5.   OCCUPATIONAL HIERARCHY

In India, the family that you are born to decides what jobs you will have. In America, Africans were forced to do the hardest, worst, and most painful jobs. Because Africans were subjected to the dirtiest and grimiest jobs, they were seen as dirty and carrying germs. Slaves were not allowed to do any work outside of farm or domestic jobs. They were not allowed to get involved in business or sales. Africans were even left out of unions in order to save jobs for white workers. America is the only country with the only culture that confines an entire caste to only 2 positions. In India, there is more variety between castes in regard to what jobs people assigned to each caste are permitted to do.

During the era of slavery, people who were enslaved were only allowed to ever show happiness. This was meant to drive up sales prices when slaves went to auction but was important for the look of slavery, the optics of it. 17 of the 20 richest black people gained their wealth through acting. Black people are phenomenal actors as they have been plastering happy faces over insurmountable grief as their children were ripped from their arms or they watched their partner get sold. They would be whipped for crying, or shouting out in pain or agony at the atrocity. When black people first began trying to make it to the big screen, a lot of them took roles as slaves but what was depicted in those movies are far from the truth. Slaves in movies are often shown as chubby which was not the case for slaves who worked on the farm. Many were often frail and thin due to their diet of corn. This was originally done as a way to further demean and embarrass black people and to reinforce their place in the society.

6.   DEHUMANIZATION

Dehumanization declares that someone is not human and it is a process that involves programming. It is hard to dehumanize a person that is standing right in front of you. Its even harder to dehumanize a person standing right in front of you who you have gotten the chance to know. It is much easier to dehumanize an entire group and it is easier to program everyone, even the targets of dehumanization, against a certain group. Caste relies on dehumanization so that any action against the disfavored caste is seen as reasonable instead of inhumane. Both Nazis and colonizers used this tactic in their adaptations of the caste system. The Nazis blamed the Jews for World War I. Not only did they blame the Jews for losing the war for them, but they also blamed the Jews for the massive amounts of debt that the country accrued during the war. Americans did the same for African Americans, blaming them for any of the problems that cropped up in the new world and any setbacks that the society endured. People were no longer individuals for individuality is the first thing lost to stigmatization. People are then lumped together as part of an animal sub-caste.

Jews and African Americans were subjected to a purposeful dehumanization. Jews were stripped of everything they owned; clothes from their past lives, head shaved, distinguishing features removed. They were no longer unique personalities to engage with but empty shells who were all the same. Nazis would force them to stand for hours, sometimes late into the night while they counted inmates. They stood in the freezing cold and in the sweltering heat. The Jews became a single mass of bodies, no longer seen a human and deserving of empathy but objects. This made it easier for the SS officers to distance themselves from their prisoners. African Americans were stripped of the names when they came to the American south and were forced to respond to new names that were meant to mock them. Jews were purposefully underfed by 200 calories so that they became weak and frail. This was used to discourage people from attempting to flee the camp or to fight back against the Nazis until they died of starvation. Both Jews and African Americans were denied protein. They were subjected to animal feed instead of food. Their captors took every chance they got to teach their slaves with food. Both dominant groups also gave the subordinate group distinctive clothing that announced their caste to others.

Any natural human reactions were not allowed to be exhibited by slaves in America. Women were not allowed to cry when their infant children were sold to other owners. Women were forced to sing cheery songs as their husbands were being dragged away or beaten in a square. Slaves were punished for the very human responses that befell them because doing so made them seem more human and less like the animals that they were often depicted as. In India, Dalits were beaten to death if they ever stole food. African American slaves were whipped for stealing food. Jews assigned to the bakery were forced to bake fresh bread for their captors while being denied sustenance. Slave auctions also became a public showcase for dehumanization. Women and men alike would be poked and prodded for hours. They were forced to answer any question that was posed to them. They had to do whatever they were told to face the whip when they returned to their homes for not selling themselves better. This just showed everyone that the dominant caste ruled and had complete autonomy over the bodies and emotions of other humans.

With dehumanization came gruesome medical experiments. Scientists and doctors had a whole pool of people who had no legal authority of their own which meant that the dominant caste could carry out horrific medical tests and trials on live humans. African Americans became a supply chain for experimentation. Scientists would torture twins, infect victims with mustard gas, or test the limits of hypothermia. All the while the enslaved patients were not given anesthesia or pain medication during experimental medical procedures. Doctors let syphilis go untreated, injected plutonium into them, and perfected the typhoid vaccine on their bodies. Doctors also began performing caesarean sections on black women as experiments as well as removing their ovaries. These doctors had unfettered access to live subjects that would otherwise have been off limits.

In an experiment looking at the threshold of violence, people were asked to deliver a series of shocks to an unknown person in the next room over. When the person administering the shocks overheard something dehumanizing about the pretend shock subject, they were willing to inflict the maximum intensity shock to those people. Dehumanization is a joint creation of biology, culture, and psychology of the mind. Unparalleled torture was applied to these groups in addition to violence, mockery that was built into the culture and society.

7.   TERRORS AS ENFORCEMENT, CRUELTY AS A MEANS OF CONTROL

In order to have a caste system that stays intact, the higher-level caste must use torture and terror in order stop resistance before it can even be imagined. Caste doesn't require white people to do anything in order for caste to function in their favor; they, instead, need to sit back and do nothing. Bystanders who do not intervene are silently complicit to those evils that they witness and do not stand up to. Yet those who join in on terrorizing the lowest caste are typically rewarded. Citizens and communities were fed a diet of hate against the Dalits, slaves, and

Jews but the subordinate caste members lived in constant fear of those above them.

Whipping was the most common form of terror and was used as much for random discretions as it was for more egregious infractions. Flogging happened to Jews in Germany but they were not permitted to exceed 25 lashes which the Jews needed to count out loud. Many Nazis skirted around this rule by alleging that they couldn't hear the Jews count their lashes or they forgot what number they were on and had to start over. In America, slaves could and would receive as many as 400 lashes and many slaves died this way.

America was the birthplace of inconceivable violence. Indigenous people were skinned alive and made into horse riding reigns. Almost any atrocity was allowed to be done to black people which meant they lived in constant fear of assaults. Slaves were burnt with branding irons that belonged on cattle. Runaways were killed or destroyed. This created such a casual disregard for black lives and the taking of those lives is still a right that many try and exercise today. Jews in labor camps were killed in front of the entire camp over the smallest infractions. Lynching in America was used in the same way, as a punishment for minor infractions or when a lower caste person acted out of their assigned place. Colonists designed a range of horrors used to keep human beings in an unnatural state of perpetual, generational imprisonment.

Slave owners even made their own slaves dish out whippings and punishment to their caste peers. This was part of the psychological manipulation used against black people. A hierarchy among captives meant that slaves had a hand in hurting their own brothers. Captives loaded their own people into gas chambers and carried their lifeless bodies out afterwards. Black people held the arms and legs of their friends and family members who were being whipped. These terrifying situations are enough to bring any one person to his knees but it was necessary to comply for survival and thus, people in the lowest caste even began to develop a mistrust for one another.

8.   INHERENT INFERIORITY VERSUS INHERENT SUPERIORITY

Caste in movies plays a big role in marking one group as inferior and the other as superior. Black women are depicted as chubby, full framed, and simple in movies while white women are shown as refined, thin, and desirable. This works to reaffirm the caste system and show that one group is always better and more preferred while black women are seen as deserving of their plight. These disparities go far beyond the movie screen and can be seen even in the most mundane interactions. Black people were prohibited from walking on the sidewalks and were only allowed to walk in the gutter as a sign of their lowly status. During the height of all caste systems, the lowest caste was not allowed to bear the symbol or status of the upper caste. In India, Dalits couldn't have clothes, homes, jewelry, of the upper caste people. In the United States, the dominant caste specified the fabrics that slaves were allowed to wear.

Some slaves who had the capacity for great intellect were sometimes subjected to live with and under masters who were unable to read or write themselves. Despite the ineptitude of their masters, slaves were expected to rely their entire sovereignty to them. Slaves were sold to drunks who beat them and sadists who mutilated them. African Americans needed to find a way to survive and avoid savage punishments while living with, oftentimes quite unstable people. African Americans were forced to shift between the ever-changing arbitrary demands of whatever dominant caste person happened to be standing in front of them at the moment and even the most trivial interaction needed to be managed with ranking in mind. In the slaveholding south, many slaves got so used to the atrocities committed against them that they wondered how they would even be after they were freed.

PART 4 The Tentacles of Caste

In 1960 there was a teacher who wanted to run an experiment with her class after the assassination of Martin Luther King Junior. The class was made up of all dominant caste members and the teacher wanted to give the students a perspective on what it might feel like to be discriminated against. She told the class that for the day, the children with brown eyes would be highly restricted and the students with blue eyes would have a lot more privilege extended to them. The teacher noticed that even in the span of the afternoon the kids who were made to feel inferior by the class took longer to complete their school work. They also exhibited less mastery over the new material taught that day. Kids who were in the more privileged group became entitled and vicious to those in the disfavored group. The teacher made the conclusion that if these circumstances are introduced to children at a young age, it will certainly impact them psychologically in ways that we may not even currently be aware of.

CHAPTER 10: Central Miscasting

At a conference discussing caste, the author noticed that she was the only person in attendance who was black. The conference spoke mostly about the plight of the lower caste people and not much about its supposed origins. Dalits were being brutalized by law enforcement in the state much like the plight of African Americans in the United States. In both cultures the lowest caste is being injured by this violence that is sanctioned by the state which harms the world.

In India, caste is everything. It is tied to religion which is why so many people looking to break free from caste denounce religion or become atheist. It is their own way of trying to escape caste. Dalits are told over and over again to be happy for their position and grateful for their plight. How and why should someone be pleased that their lot in life is predetermined from birth? Surely, caste cannot define everything that a person is and this is ultimately the reason that people hate caste. We are more than the religion we practice or the vocation that we have and when we only see someone as their caste position, you miscast the person into a role they were never meant to fill.

CHAPTER 11: Dominant Group Status Threat and the Precarity of the Highest Rung

In late 2015, the death rate of white Americans began to increase. At this same time, African American and Latinx death rates began to fall. The least educated white people began dying of suicide, drug overdose, and liver disease stemming from alcoholism or abuse. These afflictions accounted for the loss of over 500,000 white Americans. No other developed nation saw the same alarming statistics. In other places, mortality rates had fallen for the same group.

One possible reason for the change is that the wages stagnated for blue collar workers. While other western countries had also incurred stagnated wages, those other countries had more of a safety net to fall back on because their government provided certain protections that the US doesn't have. In cate terms, blue collar workers are on the lower level rung of the dominant caste ladder. For generations, they took for granted their rank in the hierarchy but there was a perceived loss of status at this time. The erosion of labor unions, fears about their place in the world, and the resentment of the reliability that their fathers could count on was now waning. It led them to question what should have been the best years of their lives.

A black president marked the inversion of the world as many had known it. This blue-collar group was the most susceptible to the call to "take the country back" or "make America great again" because this president represented a threat to their own dominant status. The disfavored group seemed to be doing too well and this threatens their place in the hierarch. The blue-collar workers are the people who, centuries ago, were enslaved by the colonial elites in the early caste system. Working class whites need the demarcation of caste in order to assert their own status. These are the people who are likely to stress aggressively that no black person will ever attain the status of even the lowest white. This is a defense mechanism to feeling threatened because they had accepted being on the bottom rung as long as they were never on the bottom.

When a hierarchy has been built around the needs of a group which one happens to be born in, it can distort the perception of one's place in the world. This creates the illusion that one is superior to others only because it has been reinforced so often that it becomes accepted as truth by the subconscious mind. Given that the hierarchy is built to serve the group by which it was created, white people have higher psychological security as a result. Civil rights era opened up the labor markets and black people faced greater competition in the workforce. Labor jobs were on the decline and the job market became tough for everyone. Groups who may have previously been seen as inferior were provided more upward mobility. Suddenly, some of those from the dominant caste found themselves lagging behind those inherently seen as inferior which launched them into existential crisis. They now seemed to share the rung with those who were supposed to be below them which meant that their own status was now lowered.

If a lower caste person moves up in the hierarchy, the higher caste person feels like they move down and equality begins to feel, to them, like a demotion. If that lower caste person surpasses an upper caste person it might feel like a threat to their very existence. Assumptions of inferiority hinder those in the lowest caste and the assumptions of superiority lie on the shoulders of those on top of the caste. They feel as though they must always stay several rungs ahead of the lowest caste, police those who dare try to cut ahead, and resent the idea that those born in the lowest caste can jump the line and get in front of those who were born to lead.

Blue-collar Americans felt like they were being slighted but we can't ignore the barrage of barriers that were flung at African Americans at this time. Government programs and protections gave white people in America a leg up. African Americans were not allowed to participate in old age insurance, labor abuse protections, and home ownership. These programs allowed white families a safety net and protections that African Americans were never affording. This has led to a wealth gap where white Americans have 10 times more wealth than their black counterparts. Rather than advocating for a deeper understanding of these disparities and how they came to be or a framework of compassion for other Americans, politics and media instead perpetuates stereotypes of black people being lazy and only looking for undeserved handouts. Once labor, housing, and schools were opened up to blacks, whites reported that they were worse off by comparison and that they experienced more racism than African Americans and unable to see the inequalities that persist in their favor.

End of the 21st century social scientists found new ways to measure what had transformed from overt racism to a slow boil of unspoken antagonisms that we now called unconscious bias. This is a discriminatory behavior that is based on prejudgments despite the person believing in equality. By adulthood, 80% of African Americans have been exposed to enough negative median of African Americans that they, too, develop a bias against themselves. This can be seen when African Americans value those with lighter skin among them. Stereotypes of blacks in the culture of society have buried themselves is deep in our subconscious minds. A pioneering study found that white felons applying for a job were more likely to be hired than black people with no criminal record. Bias against a certain group isn't always as egregious as owning slaves or waving a confederate flag. Many times, bias is quiet and insidious with many people not registering their biases in daily life. About 80% of white people are not aware of the implicit bias that shapes their behavior when interacting with a lower caste person.

There are also a great variety of disparities in the medical field. Black people are granted fewer procedures and poorer quality care than white people. Of the 60 most common procedures reimbursed by Medicare, African Americans receive fewer procedures than white patients despite higher rates of illness among African Americans. Even today, Physicians wrongly assume that black people have higher pain thresholds than white people which means that doctors do not prescribe pain medication and typically under-treat black patients. White patients typically receive pain medication when they ask for it and are even over treated. It is the overtreatment of white patients that has led to an opioid epidemic. In America's history, the government chose to criminalize drug addiction when it was ravaging black communities and yet now when white people are dying in disproportionately high numbers, the federal government steps in to render treatment and is seen as a medical problem. Preserving white life was the important decision behind the policy changes in drug treatment over the past 10 years.

CHAPTER 12: A Scapegoat to Bear the Sins of the World

Legend says that ancient Hebrews took 2 goats and presented them to the Lord. One goat they killed as a ritual sacrifice to the Lord and the other they present alive. They present the live goat only after one of the Hebrews put his hands onto the goat and imparted the sins of the village upon its shoulders. The weight and faults and insecurities were cast out into the forest on the back of a goat so that the people in town could continue to live guilt free. This goat was called the scapegoat. Now, a scapegoat has changed from the one who carries blame to the group who is blamed for misfortune. This frees the scapegoaters of their personal responsibility and strengthens the scapegoaters sense of power and righteousness.

In a caste system, the lowest level caste has historically performed the unwitting role of scapegoat by taking blame for the collective misfortune. The scapegoat helps to unify the favored caste to be seen as free of blemish as long as there is a disfavored caste to absorb their sins. A scapegoat caste has become necessary for the collective wellbeing of the castes above it. The scapegoats in America were not cast out into the forest but into the margins of society with the attempt to be banished from the human race entirely.

After the Civil War, black people were blamed for the loss of the south. People drove in from neighboring states, schools were let out early, and everyone gathered in southern towns for the lynchings that took place. The people performing the lynching never operated by themselves so that they are not seen as the one lone perpetrator carrying out these horrific fates. White solidarity was upheld and white order protected. Scapegoats are typically blamed for a crime rate they didn't cause, and for drugs that they are no more likely to use than the dominant caste and yet, thousands of black people across the country sit in jails for possession 1/8th of the marijuana or CBD that white people are now creating enterprises from growing acres of and selling.

People in the dominant caste have blamed stagnant careers and rejections in college applications on the subordinate caste and marginalized people. This, however, makes little sense. Dalits and African Americans rarely decide who gets admitted to universities or who is hired at large corporations. While affirmative action was borne out of the Civil Rights era, scholars found that it was mostly white women and, thus, white families who benefited the most from affirmative action legislation. The human impulse to blame a disfavored group puts all people in peril.

A couple from the dominant caste was driving home one evening when they stopped at a traffic light. The woman is pregnant and they are on their way home from a birthing class. A black man runs up to the window, trying to rob them when he shoots the woman in the head and the man in the stomach. The woman died but the baby miraculously lived for 17 days before perishing. The man told police that the guy who shot them was a black man wearing a jogging suit. The police sprang into action, pulling over every car and stopping to question every man they saw on the street for days. What they didn't realize in their frenzied search was that the man had just taken out a hefty life insurance policy on his wife and cashed in on it the very next day. They also didn't notice that he had been spending more and more time at the office most nights of the week. With the husband at a police lineup, he picks a random man out of the crowd and the police move to arrest him. The black man categorically denied having anything to do with the shooting. In the end, the man's brother came forward to police saying that the entire crime was an elaborate scheme to make quick money for a man who wanted to get rid of his wife. If the man's brother had not come forward with the truth, the caste system would have carried that black man all the way to jail where he would have stayed. The truth is, no one was looking at the dominant caste man for having committed such a disgusting crime. They believed that only a black man could have done it and that is what they chose to see until they had incontrovertible proof that they were wrong.

In Austin, a black man found a package on his porch when he arrived home from work. As he picked up the package, it exploded. He died quickly after making it to the hospital and the death was originally ruled as a homicide. But during a press conference, the chief of police indicated that maybe the man had been involved in a drug war or that he had made the package himself and it accidentally exploded. Crazy theories in the death of this kind man were baseless and yet, the public felt safe thinking that this was only a black people problem. The next day, a boy who lived only a short drive away found a package on his porch. He picked it up and brought it inside when it exploded and his mother was the only one who narrowly survived the bombing. Another package made its way to the home of a latinx girl. She became critically injured when she picked up a package from her moms' porch and it detonated. It took local police 10 days to make connections between all the bombings in the small city. Finally, the police were starting to take these bombings more seriously and notified the public. A bomb detonated the following day. This time, in an affluent and predominantly white neighborhood and later that day, one exploded at the FedEx store. After watching FedEx videos to see who dropped off the package, police were able to corner the suspect, Mark Conditt, in his car with a bomb on his lap. When SWAT had him surrounded, he detonated the bomb.

Blaming black people has been a long tradition in the history of our country. America constantly turns to rely on black Americans as the scapegoat for white sin. We cannot absolve ourselves by heaping our pain, blame, and problems on the backs of the people who have built this country and carried it to where it is now. In all of these examples, we can see that the people in the dominant caste who are afforded the benefit of the doubt, found a person who can be identified with evil or wrongdoing, be blamed for it, attempt to cast them out of the community in order for the remaining members to live with a feeling of guiltlessness that is the hallmark of scapegoating.

CHAPTER 13: The Insecure Alpha and the Purpose of an Underdog

The social hierarchy of wolves and dogs runs through our culture with even just our language alone. Words like; pack mentality, lone wolf, underdog, alpha male, and more are commonplace in our vocabulary today and yet, what do they really mean?

When it comes to breaking down this hierarchy, we can start at the top with the alpha male. True alphas are fearless protectors of their own pack against outside incursions. These wolves rarely use force with their own pack. A human alpha should never raise their voice and they only assert their power when necessary. Alphas are innately self-assured and inspire trust in others by watching out for everyone else. If someone steps out of line, they chastise that member with a look or a low voice but would never be caught yelling or using force. An insecure alpha will lash out at their own pack, yell, and bully their comrades into submission. An insecure alpha puts an entire pack at risk because they are showing that they lack control and that they are fearful.

What most people know about alpha males, we have learned through taking a big group of them and putting them in captivity with one another where they are forced to either fight for dominance or cower into submission. In nature; however, wolf packs are more like family units. There is both an alpha male and female that rise to their stations based on natural skill and ability. They lead with confidence and quiet assurance. At the very bottom of the pack is the omegas. These are the natural underdog of the pack and, again, get to this position based on their abilities. The omega often eats last and acts as sort of a court jester. He is picked on by other wolves but he also acts as the social glue that holds the pack together. He allows frustration to be vented at him without inciting any acts of war. When a pack loses its omega, the pack will mourn for weeks because the loss of the omega is so great.

The roles of the wolf pack are not arbitrarily defined but they are assigned with great care and purpose based on natural consequence and internal personality traits that become exposed as the pack forms. With human beings, people are prescribed alpha male status simply because they have been born to the dominant caste. This doesn't account for all those people who have the innate capacity or deservedness for leadership. Marginalized groups are forced to watch misplaced leaders fail time and time again. This deprives the world of the true alphas who can benefit societies and communities in a myriad of colorful ways when extended the chance.

CHAPTER 14: The Intrusion of Caste in Everyday Life

A black father was out to lunch with his son, knowing that he needs to have the conversation soon. The conversation about respecting authority is a conversation that only the lowest caste needs to have with their children. As a parent, it's hard to know when the time is right for these sorts of things. The sooner they know they are safer they will be but, it also robs the boy of his youth. The father could wait until the boy is older, a teenager, perhaps. But the father then worries that if he waits that long, it might be too late.

Tamir Rice was only 12 years old when he was shot and killed by police. He was a child playing in a park with a pellet gun. Lots of American boys are given water, pellet, bebe, and toy guns all of the time. Ohio is even an open carry state and, after all, this was merely a child. This boy was no different than any of the others, playing with his toy in the park. But police strode up to the park and shot him without a second thought. At some point, black boys are forced to grow up into black men far before they are ever ready and it starts when they need to confront the truth that the police will always see a threat when they see black boys and men. A boy cannot even play in the park without being targeted while doing no harm to anyone around him.

The United States has a history of the dominant caste controlling and overriding the rightful role of lower caste parents when it comes to parenting their own children. The most extreme case of this was when white slave owners would sell infants and children separate from their parents at slave auctions. Babies just born were worth $200 at their first breath and many were denied the basic human bonds with their children who were typically sold before they even finished breast feeding. Some of the most brutal whippings were dished out to enslaved men who tried to stick up for or protect their wives and children. No one was safe from the whip. No one was protected from watching it used on others.

There now exists legal and political recourse created to shield children from abuse but the hierarchy has remained intact, the modes of expression merely having mutated with the times. There are no more overt physical attacks on people of color, but attacks now are powerful enough to knock you down but invisible as they go about their work. People hold preconceived expectations about how people will interact with others based on the other person's rank. They will dismiss those who they perceive are beneath them. It is knowing, without thinking, that you are favored over others and it is reinforced by videos, movies, media, billboards, newsrooms, boardrooms, and gated communities.

Caste affects even the most ordinary of exchanges. A black woman tried to drop off a pie for her neighbor and welcome him to the neighborhood but when he opened the door, he tried to hand her his dry cleaning, simply assuming that she was there to pick up for him because he didn't assume that she lived in that neighborhood. A black college professor grabbed his mail and hopped in the elevator, joining a white man, as they made their way up to their respective floors. The professor began opening his mail when the white man in the elevator sneered at him, telling him that he should be delivering the mail and not reading it. In a third example, a contractor working on a project with two architects was told to report to a black woman with anything pertaining to a specific project. The contractor wouldn't call the black women and ended up calling the white male architect every 20 minutes with another question until the man snapped that the contractor should be calling the black female associate, not him. The contractor finally obeyed after the scolding but everyone on the project was inconvenienced by his refusal to seek the right counsel because the counsel was a black woman, someone who should be in the caste below him. In all these instances, people from the dominant caste are policing others based on the way that they look.

Another disruption to the lives of the people in the subordinate caste are when dominant caste members are constantly monitoring boundaries and disregarding the boundaries of those in the subordinate caste in order to keep the hierarchy in place. After the 2016 election, the policing of black people by white strangers became so common, these episodes have inspired memes of their own. Videos going viral of people saying racist things and coming out later to apologize. The dominant caste has been seen inserting themselves into the everyday lives of black people that they do not know and calling the police on them for doing things that are not illegal. While black people simply wait for friends outside of a Starbucks or try to enter their own apartment building, they are being surveilled. This ring a distant echo from an earlier time where white people were obligated and deputized to apprehend any black person for stepping out of line in the era of slavery. The societal interruptions of white people policing every move of black people disrupts life, responsibilities, and tears at the workings of human interactions and relationships. When you are raised middle class and born into a subordinate caste, you are keenly aware of the burden that you carry, that you must work twice as hard and know that there is no latitude for a misstep. We always make assumptions about people despite being told to never judge a book by its cover and it's time we adopt that homage as our own.

CHAPTER 15: The Urgent Necessity of a Bottom Rung

The greatest threat to a caste system is not lower caste failure but lower caste success. Achievement of the lower caste undermines the core assumptions on which the caste system was created. When marginalized people step out of their prescribed roles, people react both violently and angrily.

After the Civil War came World War I. The French asked America to join them in the war and after declining the United States finally agreed to render aid. The French was commanding American troops from both the lower and the dominant caste. French soldiers were treating people according to their military rank not their caste position. They were treating the black and white soldiers as equals, like most people would do when confronted with two human beings. The white soldiers did not like seeing the French comradery with black soldiers and even went so far as to refuse to share the trenches with them. After a battle, a few higher ranked white soldiers approached the French and asked them to stop being so nice to the black soldiers. When the French commanders gave these orders to their troops, they were met with confusion and bewilderment. The French liked the black American soldiers but the white American soldiers considered their fellowship an outrage to their national policy.

Many black soldiers died on those battlefields for France and for America. One African American soldier fought until his death, becoming wounded during the fight but refusing to back down anyways he grabbed another gun and went back out to join ranks again. Another

African American soldier led a squad that narrowed in on Hitler. Upon returning home, white soldiers nominated the two African Americans for the medal of honor. This is a major breach of the caste systems rules and norms but the men were not to be commended, even in death.

This continued during World War II. White army officers asked black army officers to direct traffic in a towns center square. When residents and other soldiers arrived, they were infuriated that a black man was telling cars when to stop and when to go. This was also a violation of caste that didn't go unnoticed by those in the dominant group. After the war was over, a black army vet who was honorably discharged boarded a bus that was traveling to his home. While the bus was driving, the veteran asked the bus driver if he could please pull over so that the man could use the restroom but the bus driver refused. The man, having been afforded a bit more freedom in the military than he would receive in the rural south, challenged the man by asking again and pleading to his humanity. The bus driver agreed and pulled over at the next stop. The veteran thought that it was his luck day. At the next stop, his luck would quickly run out. The bus driver pulled over at the next stop and called the police on the black man. The black veteran was arrested and jailed. During this arrest and in his cell, he was beaten and his eyes stabbed by the arresting officers. The next day he was charged with guilt and refused to be provided medical attention. It wasn't until 4 days later that the veteran received medical attention and by that point, his eyesight was gone and he was left permanently blind. The message was clear; that if a negro rises he must be careful not to be conspicuous.

Black efforts to rise beyond their station was met with a harsh backlash of lynchings and sparked the creation of the KKK in addition to the Jim Crow Laws of the south. All of these measures were a coordinated effort to try and keep black people in their assigned roles. In 1920, a white mob massacred 60 black people, burnt down black people's homes and businesses, castrated black men, hung people in the streets, and drove the rest of the marginalized community out of town. This was the large spark that set off a chain of anti-black rhetoric that drove people from the south to the north in the great migration. These mobs that were driving people out tended to focus their efforts on the most prosperous in the lowest caste, specifically the people who may have even surpassed some low-level dominant caste people. Black wall street was set ablaze as were the homes and churches and schools in the growing community. In another small southern town, two grocery stores stood on either end of a long block. One store was owned by a white man and the other a black man. After a small argument between boys out front, the white store owner began to harass the black store owner. The white store owner tried to intimidate the black man, showing up to the store brandishing a gun and pistol whipped him. Under the protocols of the caste system, the black man was arrested. While the store owner was in the local jail, an angry white mob went to the jail and killed him.

Thus, desperate attempts to escape caste, stigma, and prescribed social order are more likely to carry a heavier sentence than those who simply don't fight against or question the caste system. The lowest caste was to remain in its place like an ill-fitting suit. Constantly resewn to fit the requirements of the upper caste. When slaves earned money, they were seen as arrogant and vain. Black people were never credited for the ideas and innovations even when it means progress for everyone. Crediting them would mean undermining the very pretext for their enslavement, noting that their aptitude may lie in other areas which would reject the notion of their presumed inferiority in anything else but servitude.

We see this play out in the case of smallpox. When the nasty infection of smallpox began popping up in the United States, thousands of people quickly fell ill. One day while an enslaved African was talking to his owner, the African told the man about a way that his village avoided small pox at home. The slave explained that they inoculated themselves by exposing themselves to the person that was sick. The white man decided to call it variolation which is the precursor for immunization. The white man told all of his friends to try this system. The friends of his said that they weren't interested in any technique used by an African man. Those friends told others who told others who tried to burn down the white man's home. Rates of death for small pox without any treatment were 1 in every 7 people but after they were all inoculated those numbers dropped to 1 in every 40 people dying from the affliction. This knowledge was used to help save millions of lives from around the globe.

Privileges were starting to be awarded to those who fully embraced the castes system. Women in particular were starting to be trusted with more domestic responsibility and began watching and tending to the children of white women. In order to ensure that white children were not uncomfortable, white families began allowing servants in the white only sections of buses and trains when traveling with a white child. This enshrined the white child as the golden ticket to a first-class seat as a black person. This only worked to reinforce the serventile role that black women play as an integral part of the subordinate caste.

From the reconstruction era, southern school boards spent as little at 1/10th of the budget on black schools and supplies than they did for white schools. These starved children of the resources they so desperately needed to be successful in school. The board lessened the school year for black students by months so that they could spend more time in the fields. The teachers who were hired to black schools were typically under experienced and not strong teachers. The person who oversaw hiring said that they ever needed to choose between two candidates to choose the dimmer one. This was just another way to further cripple black education, punish excellence, and crush the ambition of everyone involved in this system.

The United States is fed a diet of intercity crime and poverty that is wildly out of proportion with the actual numbers that is distorts perceptions of African Americans and societal issues as a whole. Only ¼ of poor people are black and 1 in 5 African Americans are poor. Despite these statistics, a 2017 study found that African Americans account for 59% of the poor people depicted in the news. White families on the other side of the fence, make up 2/3 of America's poor but only account for 17% of the poor people depicted in the news. This old generational distortion continues to shape popular sentiment today. Crime also ends up being twisted and distorted by the media. Crimes involving a black suspect and a white victim make up 42% of crime reported on the national news despite the fact that white victims and black suspects makeup only 10%

of all crime. The culture has continued to decry the number of teenage births in marginalized communities, perpetuating the stereotype of the "welfare queen". Despite the rhetoric being around for ages, teen rates of pregnancy in communities of color has drastically dropped in the recent years. The turnaround in birth rates for teenagers has been seen in all nationalities across the board which might have accounted for the declined numbers. But that doesn't seem right. The most likely answer is that teenagers are delaying sex until they are older and/or taking more precautions when they are having sex like, using contraception correctly. Yet, these assumptions require that these girls act outside of the script assigned to their caste which is why these solutions are not figured into the equation when looking at these numbers.

Our investment in this hierarchy means that white people will sacrifice themselves in order to not allow the subordinate caste to rise. After anti-segregation laws passed, a school in the south looked for a loophole around this unfortunate development on their part. They decided that they would simply do away with school and everyone in town was forced to homeschool their children because they didn't want integrated schools. At public swimming pools that were beginning to integrate, upper caste people made it a big problem for pool managers to upkeep the pool to their likings when black swimmers would use the waters. Instead of having to deal with the integrated public schools, the dominant caste poured concrete into the pool, rendering it completely useless. The group then built a new pool behind the bars of their gated community.

CHAPTER 16: The Last Place Anxiety Packed in a Flooding Basement

Caste puts the richest and more powerful of the dominant caste at a remove. Everyone else trickles down the ladder in descending order. This puts the lowest caste into the basement with its crooked foundation and chipping cinder blocks that everyone else poignantly ignores. When those in the basement begin to rise to the other floors, the whole building is threatened. Caste pits the basement dwellers against themselves in a flooding basement that creates a panic. Those in the basement start believing that their competition is one another. They will do whatever it takes to distinguish themselves as being superior to the others on their rung, to be first and best among the lowest. The lowest caste stratifies themselves because no one wants to be in last place.

People in the lower and middle castes begin to rank themselves in proximity to whiteness and the random traits associated with it. Among marginalized Americans this meant that the closer a person is to resembling a white person in hair, eye, and skin color in addition to facial features the higher on the scale they would fall. The rape and sexual abuse of slaves in the early colonial days meant that there was a variety of skin colors and traits in the lowest caste. Those lighter skinned blacks were mean and cruel to darker African Americans in order to elevate themselves in the eyes of the dominant caste.

People hailing from the same caste system have long turned on each other in order to get in the good graces of the dominant caste. People in the lowest caste resent his peers and want to keep their peers from rising above them. Many slave rebellions or unionizing labor unions in the south were working hard to subvert these plans in an effort to maintain the hierarchy. Lower caste members who would spy on their peers and report back to the dominant caste were afforded special privileges. Their behavior maintained the system at work and the expense of progress for their brethren who simply wanted to escape and be free.

Immigrants joining the country were sure to distance themselves from the lowest caste in the basement. Again, this group worked to reject the basement caste so that they might distinguish themselves from that group as to ensure that they wouldn't suffer the same fate. All except for the black immigrants. Black immigrants from Jamaica or the Dominican Republic would be sure to keep their distinctive accents, clothing, and culture that makes them distinctly not African. These special groups of immigrants would clutch to the things that mark them as different than the Africans that were subjected to the basement. This group wasn't working to disprove stereotypes but simply wanted to announce with not so many words that they are not part of *that* group which is the worst thing that one could be.

CHAPTER 17: On the Early Front Lines of Caste

A group of anthropologists ventured down to Mississippi to undertake a mission to decode the caste system as it exists in the deep south. This was the first study of its kind and helped us to understand the realities of caste from a measured albeit subjective firsthand report of the racism that was experienced there. The anthropologists who participated in the research was a black couple and a white couple. The black couple was set to join the subordinate caste and the white couple to take their position with the dominant caste. The goal of the expedition was to understand how caste, class, and race intermingled in the antebellum south.

Many challenges befell the experiment as the couples were not permitted to spend any time together at one man's home or the other. People watched the men and the women socialize with one another despite not supposed to have known one another. Other people from the dominant caste would police their interactions which made reviewing notes and research as a team quite challenging. At one point the men needed to have a secret rendezvous where they review notes in a parked car on the outskirts of town. Even this was a risky move. If anyone discovered their meetings the experiment would certainly end or, worse yet, they could be thrown in jail or hung. Times grew tougher for black families as the research slowly drew on over the years. Both black anthropologists ended up needing to take teaching jobs in a town that was an hour drive away in order to supplement their income and keep the experiment alive.

The team found that the caste and economic systems work to reinforce each other. They documented the multiple rungs that exist between the lowest and highest castes. The researchers also detailed the social control tactics used to keep the castes separate. They documented the slave-like conditions that were forced upon farm workers and the power structure of the workers on the plantations as civilization approached the 21st century. The research also looked into the conduct required by both sides of the castes that work to maintain the hierarchy. They discussed how a black landlord needed to walk around the back of his own home in order to collect money from his tenants. They highlight the daily menace of the sharecroppers subjected to ambush whipping parties and they documented all assaults on black people.

While this team worked to conduct their research in secret, other researchers began to make their way down to Mississippi in order to observe the caste system in action for themselves. One scholar came down to the south and spent a day or two getting into the good graces of the people in the dominant caste there. On the third day the man began asking the dominant caste members who he might be able to talk to from the subordinate caste in the small town. The dominant caste members around him were disgusted, why would he want to talk to one of the disfavored castes? The man was quickly driven out of town because of the level of social scrutiny into his affairs. He quickly fell out of favor with the dominant caste which immediately crippled his status, opportunities, and research.

When the anthropologists finally wrapped up their research and sorted through everything, they had a ton of rich, accounts and information that had never been extrapolated from firsthand accounts. Despite the fact that the anthropologists were an authority on caste in the south, spoke from an immersive experience in the system, and demonstrated a mastery of the subject Davis and Gardner did not get the accolades for their project. The white man who had come to the south and published a book based on his findings while he observed the cross-caste interactions was awarded novelty for his book and accorded more authority than the other group of researchers. Resistance to the work of Allison Davis inadvertently proved the very theories that he was studying.

The concept of caste became more contentious as it was applied to American culture. The book Deep South was an irritable critique of caste in the United States. The biggest argument proposed in this book was that the caste system is singular. This is stable and unquestioned by all because even the lowest caste seemed to embrace their degraded lot as fate of the gods. The fact that black Americans resisted slavery and aspired to equality meant that caste could not be applied to this culture. If this was a true caste, Davis believed that black people would not aspire to the upper social positions held by whites. In India, these positions are not challenged and a man's caste is sacred to him. The thought is that one caste does not dominate the other in Indian caste systems. This position actively disregards the injustices inflicted on Dalits and the basic human will to be free in addition to the men who were actively fighting to be freed from the system which they were born to. In a different analysis of race, America can be clearly seen as paralleling the caste systems of India and German. The caste in America is unique to its own culture. The system here is held up by its own inertia and the dominants castes interest in upholding it.

CHAPTER 18: Satchel Paige and the Illogic of Caste

Leroy Satchel Paige was an incredible baseball player. He had a fast ball so hard that catchers had to line their mitts with steaks and extra padding to keep their hands from shattering. He didn't have the opportunity to develop as a player because he was black. This meant that he couldn't play for the major leagues and the best coaches and trainers didn't want to work with him in order to preserve their own space in the dominant caste. He was confident on the baseball field and when talking to the media that covered the black league games. He got so good at his craft of pitching by utilizing his natural talents and working his tail off. Paige was known to get to practice early and stay late to practice knocking lit cigarettes out of the mouth of his teammates. He wasn't just a strong pitcher with a killer fast ball, but he was accurate with his speed as well.

This was still at a time when the MLB was segregated and players who were from different castes were not permitted to share the field with one another. Paige was trapped playing for the black only team even though he was widely considered a superior player in the league. He never had a relief pitcher meaning that Paige pitched all game long which is unheard of in baseball today. He gave his pitches snappy names and people flooded the stands to watch him pitch. When the MLB finally integrated their baseball teams, Paige was 40 years old and he was still drafted in the league, playing with teammates who could have been his children. He was the oldest player in the league at the time and fans stormed the turnstiles to see him play. He was signed as a relief pitcher and only pitched for 2/3 of an inning and didn't allow a single hit. He pitched in the majors for a few short seasons but was old and felt as though he was on his way out.

At 59, Paige became the oldest pitcher to ever play baseball in the MLB. A team recruited Paige out of retirement as a publicity stunt. The team needed to fill stadium seats and the owner figured that Paige might make it happen. That year, Paige was signed and baseball managers and other players didn't have high expectations of him but Paige came to play. On opening day Paige threw 3 scoreless innings, leaving his team in the lead when left the mound. He knew that he deserved to be in the major leagues and that he wasn't given a fair shot. Under the spell of caste, the MLB was willing to forgo their own advancement, glory, and profits if they came at the hands of someone who should be seen as subordinate.

PART 5 The Consequences of Caste

CHAPTER 19: The Euphoria of Hate

In a 1940 silent film rolled in a museum that depicted a celebratory parade for Hitler after Germany seized Paris. People hurled confetti, hordes of women shrieked and pushed up against the body guards that were blocking off the road. The crowds were jubilant at Hitler's return from the battle and thousands of fans gathered in support and admiration for their leader. He smiled and waved at his adoring fans from a balcony that overlooked the long road littered with Swastikas and Nazi banners. The film played on a loop without commentary which made it all the more unsettling to see. What the film really showed was evil.

The Nazi party could have never risen to power and done what they did without the support of the masses and people who were open channels to his spell. Surely not all the people in the video could be evil people. They knew about the carnage for which they were celebrating. They knew Jewish friends and neighbors were round up and never to be seen again. And they were happy.

From Jim Crow Laws in the south to Dalits polluting the castes above the with nothing more than a shadow, the upper castes made sure that anyone in the lowest caste knew that they were disfavored and even hated by those in the upper castes. In all of these cultures; Germany, India, and America, a big enough majority was open to be swayed by people in power to believe that they were ordained by God to be the favored group of people. They were also convinced that these lower caste groups had been ordained by God to be subhuman.

The people in Berlin that day were neither good nor bad. They were simply human; insecure and susceptible to the propaganda that made them feel special, chosen, and important. It is hard to imagine that, if we were put in their same position, that we wouldn't do the same thing. Mere mortals find it hard to stand up to a person who acts and speaks as though they are a demigod. A demigod who makes you feel better about yourself, makes you feel part of something bigger than yourself. Both rhetoric are ones that these people have been primed for and were ready to fully believe.

Many of us say that we would never commit such atrocious acts against our fellow humans and yet, thousands of people did. This was the result of the buildup of insecurities and resentments over many years. Some of the witnesses and participants in both the Nazi party and slave ownership are still alive today. Germany taught the world that evil does not belong to one person. But that evil can be activated in more people than we want to believe when the right conditions congeal. It is easy to simply ask to root them all out, the bigots and the evil people but that is not realistic because those things exist in all of us, lying dormant. We cannot wait for these people to die either. The threat is not one man, but all of us. Lurking in humanity itself.

CHAPTER 20: The Inevitable Narcissism of Caste

Through no fault of the ppl born to it, the dominant caste acts as the sun around which all other castes revolve. Defines it as the default setting standard for intellect, beauty, normalcy against which all others are measured and ranked in order by their proximity to the dominant caste. Dominant caste is depicted as hard working and superior in all aspects of life. Society built a trap door of self-reference that unwittingly forces them to take on narcissistic isolation from those who are assigned to lower categories. This replicated the structure of narcissistic family dynamics with the interplay of competing, supporting roles. There is the middle child caste that tries to vie for attention from the narcissistic parent. The lost child of the caste would allude to the indigenous people who were cast out of society completely. Finally, there is the scapegoat child made up of the slaves in the caste system. The centrality of the dominant caste is not lost on those who belong to other castes. The highest and lowest rung are so far apart that the rungs seem immovable. This results in the middle group feeling as the most uncertainty as they aspire to a higher rung.

Those who are accustomed to being the standard against which human beings are measured. They always have the assurance that while they have hardship and troubles but at least they will never be at the bottom. As long as the bottom dwellers stay in their place, their own identities and futures are secure. White people will always have comfort after being convinced since birth that they have superior blood, genes, and intellects. Locking the subordinate caste into their bottom rung has always afforded the dominant caste solace in a stressful and fluctuating world.

Narcissism is a complex condition and can be applied to the nature of tribes, nations, and communities. Narcissism was first unearthed in the story about the Greek god, Narcissus, who was so caught up in staring at his own reflection and trying to kiss it that he fell into a lake and drowned. Narcissism is when a person or group is caught in the illusion of loving one's self too much. We see narcissism in groups that have been trained to believe in their inherent sovereignty, hate all those that are different from them, and overestimate one's own power, abilities, and position in society. A narcissistic leader is nothing. But if he can identify with his nation or transfer his personal narcissism to the group, then he is everything.

A narcissistic leader is a person who is deeply invested in their group's dominance. This type of leader gives off energy as if they are on top of the world when in reality they are in a state of self-inflation which leads to a severe distortion in that person's capacity to judge right from wrong, or good from bad. This leader makes sure that he and his are overvalued while everything outside is grossly undervalued. Underneath the charisma and self-confidence lies fear. Fear that one cannot live up to the constructed ideal of his own perfection. The disease of narcissism is so damaging that people will conquer, colonize, enslave, and kill their fellow humans in order to maintain their illusion of natural superiority. When under threat, these groups are willing to sacrifice themselves in order for the group to survive because it is from the survival of the group that one draws their self-esteem. Their investment in this illusion gives them as much of a stake in making everyone beneath them to feel inferior as they have in making themselves appear superior.

CHAPTER 21: The German Girl with the Dark Wavy Hair

During World War II, Jews had all but vanished from German life. Without a scapegoat to look down upon, the people had only themselves to regard and distinguish them from the other. The fixation on purity put everyone on high alert. During this tense time, a person in town made an offhand remark about a young girl who lived just outside of town. Something about her appearance made people double take as she walked by. Of course, the people in the village noticed that the girl's hair was darker than most. Hitler himself had dark brown, almost black hair. But the hair that sat atop his head was decidedly straight and fine. The girl in the village had hair that was thick and wavy. People began to speculate that maybe there was Persian in her family line, or perhaps she had a distant relative hail from the middle east.

People increasingly became more aware of the girl's hair and openly began making comments about it. Now that the villagers were looking at the girl they began to notice that her skin was a bit off color as well. It wasn't the ruddy or yellow undertones that most Germans seemed to possess, but she had a slightly olive complexion. Her skin tone even began to stand out among her own family members. It is these types of tiny, minute details and distinctions that take on a much larger significance when there are less distinctions to make. Under the Nazi party, these distinctions carried greater consequences than mere idle chatter among villagers. This was an explosive observation that could have cost the little girl her life.

The young girl began to stare at herself in the mirror, matching her features up with photographs of Arian women. She measured her forehead, the length of her eyes, and the width and length of her nose to see if her features fell within an arbitrary range made up by the dominant caste to impose stark boundaries regarding who could be considered Arian and who would not be. The family, overcome with anxiety, began discretely combing their family tree in an effort to unearth any disfavored lineage in their family's ancestry to no avail. The girl ultimately lived through the war, but she was forever tainted by the experience. Even the favored ones were diminished and driven to fear in the shadow of supposed perfection.

CHAPTER 22: Stockholm Syndrome and the Survival of the Subordinate Caste

People who live at the margins of society had to study those at the center of power because their survival depends on knowing them better than knowing their own needs and wishes. From the sidelines, they learn to be watchful of the needs and tempers of those in the dominant caste. Knowledge without wisdom is adequate for the dominant caste but wisdom is essential to the survival of the subordinate caste. To thrive, subordinate caste members must constantly adjust themselves to the random and arbitrary expectations of whatever upper caste person confronted them. They need to figure out what their role is any given situation and play their part. While people in the subordinate caste may not choose to fully submit to the expectations of the dominant caste, many find it much easier to stick to the script that has been provided to them through the ages. If those in the subordinate caste choose to accept their roles, their first moral duty is to resign to the expectations of the favored caste. The subordinate caste must not only monitor the safety of themselves through their own eyes but also adopt the perspective of the higher caste person. The dominant caste demands that the subordinate caste extend them compassion that has never been extended in the other direction. These rival expectations of being subordinate but also being forced to see through another perspective and extend that person's empathy brings up the theory of Stockholm Syndrome.

This syndrome has no universal definition or diagnosis but is generally seen as a syndrome in which people bond with those that abuse them or hold them hostage. The syndrome was named after an occurrence that took place in Stockholm, Sweden. A bank robber kept a group of people who were in the bank as hostages. After a 7-day standoff, many of the hostages had begun to empathize with their captor and even felt bad for him. This is thought to be due to the survival mechanisms that kick in when people are worried for their lives. People become attuned to the people who have power over them and learn to adjust themselves in order to please their captor or abuser in order to remain safe.

In Dallas, a white former police officer was found guilty of shooting and killing a black man who was in his apartment alone. He was watching television, eating pizza and ice cream. The man was doing nothing wrong and didn't even have the chance to talk through the misunderstanding with the woman who shot him dead. The woman claims that she entered the wrong apartment and, thinking that the apartment was hers and shot the supposed intruder. The conviction carried a maximum sentence of 90 years. The prosecutor recommended 28 years, which would have been how old the victim was at the time of the sentencing had he not been killed. The former officer was ultimately sentenced to 10 years in prison with the possibility of parole in only 5 short years.

After the sentencing concluded, the slain man's brother publicly hugged the former police officer who happened to be from the dominant caste. He told the woman that he forgave her for her negligence in killing his brother. Their shared hug went viral on the internet. After the sentence was rendered, a bailiff who came from the subordinate caste approached her and began stroking her hair and the women curled up like a child into the bailiff's bosom. Even further still, the judge who was also a subordinate caste member, left the bench and gave the former police officer a bible and, together, prayed over it. Why would it seem that these subordinate caste members would be consoling and extending forgiveness to a woman who shot and killed a person of their own caste in cold blood, without even a moment to allow him to explain himself. Without a second for him to ask what she was doing in his apartment.

These embraces seemed not far removed from the comfort black maids extended to the sad white children left in their care; wiping away their tears over the centuries. No such compassion would ever be extended to a black person who had just been convicted of shooting and killing a member of the dominant caste in cold blood. Around the same time the dominant caste woman was being corralled into the warm embrace of forgiveness after murder, a 21-year-old black man in Florida was having a starkly different experience. The black man was sentenced to 10 days in jail because he arrived late to jury duty. There was no compassion shown to this man who had the entire weight of the law thrown at him instead of showing him kindness and forgiveness. The man was the only black man that was serving on the jury and he was not only singled out but also held to a different standard than any of the white jurors who he was serving with. The man had no criminal record until this incident and the judge made sure that his transgression would stay with him for the rest of his professional, adult life.

In 2014, the country erupted with protests in response to the death of an 18-year-old black man who was shot and killed by police in Ferguson,

Missouri. At one of the protests, a boy in the front of a large crowd of protestors stood pointing a sign that read "free hugs" at police officers standing only a short distance away. Something about the still image struck the author wrong. The boy's face looked weathered and inexplicably mournful. A police officer approached the boy and they shared an embrace that brought tears to the boy's eyes, streaming down his face as people snapped photographs that instantly went viral after this period of racial tension. What was the tragedy beneath the moment of apparent pain and reconciliation?

The black boy from the heartbreaking photograph in Missouri lived with two white women who had adopted him and several other black children. Over the course of 10 years, the two women from the dominant caste essentially held the children captive. The women kept the children in total isolation and fed them meager crumbs. They were beaten with belts and the women's fists. The women would use them as props to attract a social media following. They would make them dance and sing, virtually performing for them and the rest of the world while being denied a normal childhood existence. When the children sought help or food from teachers or neighbors, the women ordered others not to intervene and help the children. The women used their power and status to deflect investigations into the wellbeing of the children by telling other people that all of the children were crack babies, that they're mentally unwell, and lie all the time. People saw what they wanted to see and every time an investigatory adult would come knocking, the family would simply pick up and move to a different jurisdiction. When a California case worker began to close in on actual abuse allegations, the women packed up their van with all their children in tow and drove it over a California cliff.

Black forgiveness of dominant caste sin has become a spiritual form of needing to be twice as good in trauma and all other aspects of life to be seen as half as worthy. There is a societal expectation that subordinate caste members bear their suffering and absolve the people who brought that harm against them. White people love to embrace narratives of forgiveness after the massacre so they can pretend the world is a fairer place than it is and racism is only a thing of the past and not the present. Black people are expected to forgive in order to survive in a white dominated world. When the shoe is on the other foot, white silence in the face of racism has continued to thrive and is a hallmark of the caste system at work. Black people have had to endure generational slavery, segregation, lynching, Jim Crow laws, inequality in every realm, and mass incarceration yet those who have always harmed black people continue to do so.

A woman in Brooklyn accused a 9-year-old black boy of sexual assault and called the police on him. The little boy, scared and confused, was crying and repeating his innocence. The woman, a member of the favored caste, maintained her story. It wasn't until the police pulled the security camera footage that the woman and the world witnessed the boy's bag, not his hand or shoulder nor any body part, brushed up against the woman. The shame of the video forced the woman to issue an apology to the boy. White people waited expectantly, wanting to know whether or not the boy forgave the women. The dominant caste was looking to be released of all guilt in this moment of social error but the boy, still unaware of the workings of the caste system and roles of people in a caste, announced that he did not forgive her. He even went on to say that he thought she needed help. What white people are asking for when they make calls for forgiveness is a pardon. They want absolution from the racism that affects us all. Even though forgiveness alone cannot reconcile America's racists sins.

CHAPTER 23: Shock Troops on the Border of Hierarchy

It was time to eat on a 19th century steamboat in the antebellum south but there was still a caste order that needed to be upheld. The hierarchy began with the white passengers. The dominant caste people were to eat first while seated with the ship's captain. After they were done, a bell rang and the white crewman and servants sat for their dinner. Only after all of the white passengers had eaten, did the final bell ring for the black passengers to sit for dinner. The black passengers, who bought the same tickets as the white people who dined with the captain, ate with the black crewman and servants. The black people who bought their middle-class tickets were still not afforded the privilege of sitting their people who are in their class, but were forced to resign to their caste status; eating white standing in the pantry huddled over a small table.

Free blacks were the largest affront to the caste system, moving as equals to the dominant caste and having the ingenuity to gain freedom through the entire caste system into question. If people in the lowest caste had the capacity to be equal with white people, why were they being enslaved? If these people were able to do something other than pick cotton or scrub floors than why were these the only jobs afforded to these people?

Since the start of the caste system, any minority who dared to rise above their station in the hierarchy have been the shock troops in the line of the hierarchy. People who appear in places or positions that are unexpected for a person of their caste, became foot soldiers in a war of gaining respect and legitimacy in a fight they hoped was long over.

Public and recreational spaces became a test of caste when people were forced to interact across caste levels.

A group of women from the subordinate caste had joined a wine tour. The women were laughing and chatting as many other passengers on the train were doing with their respective groups. The employee on the train approached them and told them that their laughing was making other passengers uncomfortable. The women weren't doing anything wrong or breaking any rules but the train stopped and the women were forced off the train. The police were even called, one woman complaining that they women were acting crazy. Another instance occurred in 2018 when a group of subordinate caste members were playing a round of golf at a country club. The women, experienced golfers by their own admission, timed their game so that they weren't too close to the group in front and they had been sure to keep tabs on the group behind them so as not to hold them up. Yet, the dominant caste men who were playing behind the subordinate caste women called the owner of the country club and said the women were playing too slow. The men behind them hadn't even been playing, but were sitting and taking a break. The police were called and found that no crime was committed but the women packed up and left the course regardless.

The author recounts a story in which she is in the airport and is getting ready to board her flight with first class. She had just injured her wrist and knew that she would need help putting the bag in the overhead compartment. As she got onto the plane, she asked the flight attendant, a dominant caste man, if he could help her with the bag since her wrist was in a splint. The man dismissed her, telling her that an attendant in the back of the plane would help her. Isabel sheepishly told him that she was, in fact, sitting in first class. Another flight attendant came to her rescue but that didn't stop the male flight attendant from giving her annoyed glances and curt conversation when taking her drink order. Things escalated when the men seated behind Isabel began heckling her when she attempted to recline her seat to sleep on the plane. The grown men from the dominant caste hit the back of the seat repeatedly so that she was forced to sleep cross country sitting upright. Not one of the several white people in first class, or on the plane even came to her aide.

Caste works smoothly when people don't speak up or intervene when they witness treatment like this against people who belong in the subordinate caste. White people hardly step to the aid or defense of black people which only strengthens the system further. Incursions like these are more than misunderstandings or personal insults. Fighting convention, fighting to be seen and treated for who you are diminishes the nature of human relationships. It demeans everyone. It worsens the wellbeing of all people. A lot of these instances end in violence when people do stand up to the caste system which is a hallmark of caste at its breaking point.

CHAPTER 24: Cortisol, Telomeres, and the Lethality of Caste

A young man immigrated from Nigeria to the United States in order to pursue college when he was just 17. The boy went to the bursar's office to receive a refund check when the woman there made a comment that he spoke very good English. He was appalled at the comment and promptly told the woman that of course he spoke great English. He spoke several languages fluently and didn't need her approval. He quickly discovered that, in America, he would never be seen for his intellect or skills. They only saw the color of his skin which provided them all the information they feel as though they need to know. He knew that African Americans were always being profiled and mistreated but he didn't know the extent of it until he was experiencing it all for himself. He could see the hierarchy in the way women clutch their pearls when he walked by. He saw it when the lady that pulled up next to him at a traffic light locked her car door to which he responded by promptly locking his. He saw it in the way he was passed over for a promotion at his job despite his experience and seniority.

Modern medicine has long sought to attribute higher rates of disease, high blood pressure, and diabetes to genetics of those who are most afflicted, which is African Americans. What is interesting though, is the fact that sub-Saharan Africans do not have high rates of high blood pressure, heart disease, or diabetes. This leads science to consider something else entirely as the cause of these health disparities. We have discovered that it is the friction of caste that is killing people. Social inequality is killing people. The act of moving about and navigating spaces with whom society has trained us that we are inherently subservient to is killing people and not just the targets.

Prejudice itself can affect people's health. Scientists found that harboring this animosity towards others can raise blood pressure, and cortisol levels even during benign social interactions with people of different races. These physical reactions can put the person at greater risk of stroke, diabetes, heart attacks, and premature death. A study of white Americans who scored high on a measure of automatic prejudice found that when they were put into situations where they were interviewed for a job by an African American, and had a social interaction with latinx people, they perceived the people of a different ethnicity as a threat. The threat that they perceive as a result of their prejudice set off their bodies alarm system, their panic produced automatic bodily responses as would occur as if they were in combat or confronting an oncoming car. The effects of the prolonged stress under the caste system is highly damaging to the heart and immune system on a regular basis.

Even looking at a faded yearbook picture of a black person can trigger this response in white people within 30 milliseconds of exposure which is as fast as a blink of an eye. When whites have more time to allow their conscious mind to override the initial reaction of threat, the amygdala switches to inhibition mode. When white people see a human being with their own individuality and personal characteristics, the threat level falls. This shows that it is possible to overcome these physiological responses, our worst impulses, and reduce these prejudices. In order to overcome this programming, people need to work on diverse teams for a common goal, teams that require cooperation in order to succeed.

For lower caste people, scientists have made a discovery that can allude to a person's health and longevity with the science of telomeres. Telomeres are a repeating sequence of double strand DNA that appears at the end of a chromosome. The more frequently a cell divides, the shorter the telomeres. The constant dividing of cells leads to a phenomenon called "weathering" which is a measure of premature ageing. This premature cell ageing makes African Americans more susceptible to diseases and aliments. Expanded research finds that this damage results from social inequities, discrimination, and difficult life conditions rather than race or ethnicity. Thus, the telomeres of poor whites are shorter than affluent whites whose resources might better help them weather life's challenges.

The opposite is true for those in the lowest caste. Prosperity, wealth, and the assumed privilege that comes with it does not protect the health of well-to-do African Americans. In fact, many suffer a health penalty for their ambitions. Middle class African Americans are more likely to suffer from hypertension and stress than those with lower incomes. The stereotypes that they live under expose them to higher levels of stress inducing discrimination in spite of their perceived educational or material advantages. High levels of everyday discrimination can lead to the narrowing of arteries over time, higher levels of inflammation which is a marker of heart disease. This leads to premature death and can be seen in all people of all ethnicities based on their experiences with discrimination.

When it comes to life expectancy, middle age and less educated Americans are experiencing a downward trend, as we observed. Yet ppl of color at the bottom of the caste, still have an overall lower life expectancy than their white counterparts at every level of education. The average white American at age 25 is likely to live 5 years longer than a black American. White high school dropouts have a shorter life expectancy than their more educated counterparts, still live 3 years longer than African American dropouts. White college grads live 4 years longer than African American college grads. People of color with the most education who compete in fields where they are not expected to constantly push up against the boundaries of caste and experience a lower life expectancy as a result. The caste system will literally take years off the life of the subordinate caste system when people fight to break free of the caste system that confines them.

PART 6 Backlash

CHAPTER 25: A Change in the Script

Electing an African American to the office of president meant that the caste system was turned on its head. History had shown that there would be consequences to the social order as a result and indeed there was. To break the 2 centuries long tradition, the country needed a president who was spotless and manicured as well as even-keeled and intelligent. Obama was a Harvard trained lawyer, a US senator, a person whose expertise was the constitution itself. Obama spoke to the heart of people, saying that he saw the country as the United States rather than as blue and red. His wife was also a Harvard trained lawyer and the two of them, in addition to their vice president, ran a flawless campaign. Obama proved to be an idealist who truly believed that it was possible to make his dream come true.

From a caste perspective, Obama's origin story was one that the system was ready to accept. He grew up in Hawaii and did not grow up with Jim Crow so he didn't have to surmount Jim Crow laws and his story freed the dominant caste from having to think about the unsavory corners of American history. People from the dominant caste could claim him as part of themselves because his mother and grandmother were white. People were relieved to say that racism is a way of the past and yet a majority of white voters did not support him in either of his presidential bids. No matter how refined or inspirational he was, Obama's victory did not occur because white people became enamored with him. He won despite the bulk of the white electorate. 3 out of 5 voters did not vote for him in his first election. In Mississippi, only 1 in 10 white voters voted for Obama.

For many, Obama's victory signaled that the dominant caste would be facing a wane in power. McCain's loss was a profound loss to white status. No one from the dominant caste had ever needed to contemplate this before, forced to consider the loss of their centrality. The dominant caste would not allow this violation of the hierarchy go unanswered. The caste system sprang to action in order to protect the existing order. The republican party couldn't keep Obama from a second term but worked tirelessly to obstruct every proposal he made and resorted to executive orders to accomplish his aims. People began to question Obama's legitimacy as a US resident and the 'birthers' began a tireless crusade to prove that Obama was not born in the US, asking him, repeatedly, to produce his birth certificate. Even after he did, they still were not satisfied and continued their damaging rhetoric.

Contrary to the wistful predictions of racial harmony, the number of hate groups surged from 602 to more than 1000 in the middle of Obama's first term in office. A 2012 survey found that anti-black attitudes and racial stereotyping rose instead of fell during Obama's first term. Explicit anti-black attitudes moved from 48% in 2008 to 51% in 2012. Implicit bias rose from 49% to 56%. Findings included higher percentages of white respondents found that they saw African Americans as violent, irresponsible, and lazy after Obama's victory despite the wholesome black family in the white house with two ivy league parents. Attacks on African Americans worsened in the reversal of the hierarchy.

CHAPTER 26: A Turning Point and the Resurgence of Caste

The election was the biggest thing that happened in 2016. The Republican nominee was already disregarding time honored norms like blowing off major debates in the primaries. Our country watched as a presidential candidate boasted about grabbing women by the genitals, mocked a disabled reporter, ridiculed the grieving parents of an American war hero who was Muslim, and demeaned another war hero, John McCain, for getting captured by the enemy before escaping and getting rescued. Good people of this country watched as the country prepared to turn itself back on its head. And it was not going to be pretty.

No aspect of American life can be fully understood without considering caste and the embedded hierarchy. Many people didn't think a Trump win was possible. They didn't believe that working, middle class whites would vote directly against their interests in supporting a right-wing oligarch but that theory diminishes the agency of the dominant caste and the long-term goal of preserving one's own place in the dominant caste and the survival of white supremacy. Trump also channeled insecurities and disaffection that went deeper than economics. White voter's preference for Trump was related to their own survival and job security. People feared that minorities were going to replace them in the caste system. This is why racial attitudes are a culprit in changes of white partisanship. Researchers called this group hypervigilance phenomenon racialized economics. The belief that other racial groups are getting ahead while your group is falling behind. The changing demographics of the country induced a greater need to maintain the advantages that they have come to expect and to shore up the immutable characteristic that has always held the most weight in the American caste system. White racial solidarity influences whites' political attitude and behavior. Many whites are looking to reinforce a social order in which their group is firmly at the top.

The 2016 election became a broken mirror for the country that had not been forced to look at its origins for more than a generation and see ourselves for what we really are. The stigma and double standard attached to racial minorities have amassed to the democrats while the privilege and latitude accorded to the dominant caste have gone to the republicans who have become representations for white America. Most white women in the 2016 election completely disregarded the common needs of women and went against a fellow white woman to vote for the white side of their identities to which Trump appealed. People align themselves with a candidate whose power and privilege intersect with the trait of their own. The majority of people will vote up in caste, or across caste, but won't vote down the caste rung. Once in office, Trump has made clear that he would work to undo everything that Obama worked so hard to put in place because protecting their hierarchy and regaining a sense of dominance trumps social, economic, and personal wellbeing.

CHAPTER 27: The Symbols of Caste

Robert E Lee, the confederate general in favor of slavery, was given a statue in Charlottesville, VA but was covered in a black tarp. City leaders didn't know what to do with it. In the previous weeks, white supremacists had turned violent in the city's plan to remove the statue. It was as if the passions of the civil war had been resurrected. On that day in 2017, swastikas and confederate flags they chanted anti-Semitic and racists things as they marched through a college campus, finally gathering in the square where the statue sat. armed republicans joined the protest rally as it grew. This drew counter protests of peace from the opposition that ended with a white supremacist driving a car through the center square, injuring many and killing a lawyer who came to try and instill peace.

The 13th amendment ended slavery but it left a loophole where the dominant caste were able to enslave African Americans who had committed a crime. This led the dominant caste to arrest people of the subordinate caste for things like; loitering, or vagrancy. This happened just as the North began to pull back from their oversight of the south, pulling its occupying troops out and leaving the slaves unprotected with the people who had enslaved them and their families for generations. This led to a mutation in slavery called sharecropping that was basically slavery with new conditions and a new name.

The South had lost the war but they still had plenty of money from their booming agriculture investments. The southern generals and their supporters began erecting statues everywhere to commemorate the slave holders and reinforce or forewarn the lowest caste of their lowly status and powerlessness. People who had lived through floggings, lynching's, family displacement, and more tragedies were now forced to stare up at the monuments of the men who inflicted harm against them and their families. If the south lost the war, the culture and treatment of the lowest caste did not reflect it. The return to power of the confederates meant that there would be retribution for those who had fought against them.

Robert E Lee believed that slavery was more of a problem for the owners than the victims and truly thought that black people were far better off as American slaves than free Africans in their home country. This is the man who led the confederate trooped into a losing batter in order to continue the inhuman act of owning another human being. All across the south in both grand and innocuous places, there are more than 100 monuments dedicated to Robert E Lee. Schools, plaques, parks, national forests, are a few of the institutions that bear the slave owners name. Normally it is the victors of a war who erect monuments of themselves in their honor. In this instance, an outsider might not be able to tell which side prevailed over the other.

As racial tensions grew over the past several years, many cities and towns all over the country began to regard their civil war relics with disdain. Local officials in the south have tried to remove inflammatory monuments for slave owners. This has been met with violent backlash all around the country. People blowing up the cars of the construction companies invited to take on the project, sending them death threats. As workers took down the monument that sat in a New Orleans square, onlookers flew drones and took pictures, trying to identify the workers through their masks and long sleeve shirts. The men had to be covered head to toe for their anonymity and protection. SWAT sat perched on rooftops, keeping a valiant watch over the removal efforts in case the violence began to rear its ugly head.

Across the ocean, Germany erected a statue in memorandum for the Jews who lost their lives in the concentration camps. All Jews who lost their lives in a concentration camp were honored somewhere in the city. Micro-memorials also contain the names of holocaust victims. The micro-memorials are beautiful gestures called stumbling stones that have been placed all across Europe. They are embedded in cobblestones in front of apartment buildings where Jewish citizens had been known to live before being whisked off to die in concentration camps. These stumbling stones force the viewer to pause and go for a closer look. Each one is a personal headstone that gives a moment of connection to an individual person who has a long past but remains a sacred part of German history. Leaning over to look at the stones forces viewers to bow in respect.

Germany has no monuments that celebrate the Nazi armed forced no matter how many grandfathers fought or fell for them. Instead, they made memorials for those who resisted the Nazi influence and died during this terrible period. In Germany, displaying a swastika is a crime. City officials quite literally paved over Hitler's grave. No resident in Germany is expected to run or hide from these atrocities that took place on German soil but, instead, seek to discuss it and memorialize it. This means that they don't wince or look away from their history but face this darkness every single day in memorial to ensure that it never happened again.

CHAPTER 28: Democracy on the Ballot

In the summer of 2014 heading into 2015, there were waves of videos being released of police shooting unarmed black men. People began organizing and protesting, yelling from the streets that black lives matter. The confederate flag was finally taken down in Colombia, Maryland and it appeared that, for a moment, the country had removed its mask. Some political analysts believe that this was a moment of truth. Maybe, the country needed to be unmasked in order for real change to start happening, for real healing of this fractured land to take place. But the recoil was painful and showed us all that our country still has a long way to go.

The shooting of Treyvon Martin marked the start of 21st century backlash. Grandfather clauses faded so now, states were shutting down polling stations early, rejecting voter identification over a misplaced apostrophe, and purging voter registrations. A shooting of an unarmed black man by police went without prosecution. All of these tactics used to keep black people in their assigned place in the hierarchy. Instilling fear and uncertainty back in the hearts and minds of all citizens who walk through this world. Trump brought to the surface what had been there all along, meaning that it should make it easier for us to defeat.

CHAPTER 29: Price we Pay for Caste

America can be a harsh landscape, a less benevolent society than other developed, wealthy nations but this is the price we pay for our caste system. In places with a different hierarchy it is not seen as taking away from one's own prosperity if the system looks out for the needs of everyone. People show a greater sense of joint responsibility for one another when they see their fellow citizens as humans like themselves. They feel as though everyone had equal stake in the lives of their fellow citizens. There are other thriving, prosperous nations in which people don't need to go into great debt or sell their most valuable possessions to receive medical care. Places where families don't go broke while taking care of elderly loved ones and children can exceed the educational achievements than Americans, and addiction is met with treatment instead of imprisonment and happiness & a long life is the standard because they are focused more on their commonality than their differences.

A caste system builds rivalry, distrust and lack of empathy toward one's peers instead of harmony. The result is that the United States lags in major indicators in quality of life more than any other developed country in the world. The US has the highest incarceration rate in the world. We imprison more people than any other nation, 2.2 million people to be exact. American women are more likely to die during pregnancy & childbirth than any other nation. In the developed Western world, there are 14 deaths per 100,000 live births which is nearly 3 times the rate in Sweden. Infant mortality in the US is the highest among the richest nations. Life expectancy in the United States is the lowest out of the 11 richest countries in the world. The average person in America lives 78.6 years compared to an average of 82.6 years out of all developed states and, finally, the highest life expectancy rate, 84.2 years in Japan. American students score near the bottom in industrialized nations in math & reading. The scores of the students fall below the scores of both Latvia & the Czech Republic. By the time a woman ran for major office in America during the 2016 election, 60 other countries had already had a women head of state. The US ranked 18th in happiness in the world, just above the Czech Republic but has fallen 7 spots since 2012, showing our growing discontents.

After all these negative shifts, America caught wind of the coronavirus spreading out of an epicenter in Beijing, China. The Earth's most powerful nation diluted itself into believing that American exceptionalism would mean that America was safe from the effects of the incoming pandemic but that fading hope was quashed when the pandemic made its way into American homes, businesses, and schools. Quickly, America had the largest coronavirus outbreak in the world. As the virus made its rounds in the United States, it would be America's African American and Latinx communities that began dying at higher rates. Preexisting conditions from the stresses of marginalized life factored into most of these deaths. To the rest of the world, absence of affordable health care, competition for scarce medical supplies that pit states bidding against one another, chaotic social distancing rules, and the clear lack of a centralized response made America look weak instead of the like powerhouse we should be. This was a failure of character more than anything else in American history. It dehumanized others to build civilization and now it needs to find its own.

PART 7 Awakening

CHAPTER 30: Shedding the Sacred Thread

A boy born into the upper caste of India has 2 births. One birth from his mother when he enters the physical plane, and the other when he is initiated into Brahman manhood. During the Brahman initiation ceremony, a thread is placed over the head and sits on the shoulders of the boy being initiated. The thread is never to some off for any reason and if it becomes dirty or impure, it must go through a sacred cleaning. One day, the boy watched as his father walked past a neighbor on his way to town. The neighbor, a Dalit, didn't down to the boy's upper caste father. The father chased the Dalit down but the man simply hid behind a tree branch. The boy's father should have slapped him, should have forced him to bow. But the father... didn't. Instead the father retreated and vacated the village. All of the other Brahman found out and the boy's father had shamed their family, their name, and their caste by letting the Dalit disrespect him in that way.

The boy grew up and had a family of his own but grew up to see the inequalities around him. He knew that the lower level castes did not accept their lot. He also knew that Dalits were not the lazy, docile, creatures that have been born of caste fantasy. He came to realize that the Dalits were just as capable as he was and many of them had world experience that he was not afforded from his comfortable upbringing. Creativity & intellect were not designated to one caste alone, he learned. He came to see what had been lost by one not getting to know the people from other castes; who they are, their likes and dislikes, their goals and dreams. The boy realized that he had been told a lie and trying to live up to the lie destroyed the boy's father.

The boy finally decided to remove his threat. It was a toxic snake around his neck. Removing it meant that the boy was rejecting his family, his caste, and his religion. The boy was now born a third time. The boy woke up to realizing that caste is artificial and the disregarding caste means embracing who you really are instead of being who the caste system asks you to be.

CHAPTER 31: The Heart is the Last Frontier

The month was December in the year 2016. It had been one month since the election. The author had called a plumber in order to help her with a flood in the basement. A plumber wearing a MAGA cap waddled up to Wilkerson's home, standing at the threshold of the front door. The plumber looked surprised to see a black woman open the door in a primarily white neighborhood. White women in ponytails pushed strollers, lawn service workers tended to other people's lawns, maid vans were parked up and down the street.

Now that Isabel was widowed and motherless, she needed to depend on contractors and another vocational ppl to help fix the house. It's always a risk, bringing in a plumber who she didn't know. Maybe they won't help. Maybe they will make things worse. She can never be sure.

He seemed annoyed with her and short of patience when he entered the basement. Before the plumber came, an immigrant man came to inspect the HVAC and helped drain the water which Wilkerson told the man. The plumber stood there, watching Isabel shuffle boxes and sweep up water but didn't do anything to help the flood in her basement. He didn't even try to fix anything for her.

It was only after Wilkerson appealed to his humanity, the man started to try and help by doing his job. They spoke about their deceased mothers and the feeling of grief that they both felt when they lost them. They shared tidbits about their families and it seemed, for a moment, they were able to find common ground, the stand on where they could clearly see eye to eye. The plumber began to clear the sump pump. He helped move boxes to find the drain in order to make sure it wasn't clogged. Finally, he inspected the whole basement to find that the water that flooded the basement came from the water heater. How different things had been since they took a moment to connect as human beings. He shut off the water heater to stop the flooding & gave her an estimate for a new one.

CONCLUSION

Caste is a figment of our imagination, based on physical traits that are inherently immutable and unchangeable, giving caste it's fixed structure. This determination was made so far back in our collective history it has been made to seem like the natural order of the world at large. It has made its way into every corner of American life and is continuously perpetuated in order to halt progress on true equality.

It is imperative to examine the history and origin of caste systems on a macro scale, looking to countries like India and Germany to help us understand the framework in which caste operates as well as the tell-tale markers of a caste system at play. America may have learned or garnered a lot of caste structure from India but it was Germany who looked to borrow the notions of caste during the Nazi party's rise to power. If we don't truly understand the horrors of our history, the nation will never be able to move past the terrors that were inflicted on the subordinate caste we must, first, face them. While many people are quick to brush slavery and the Jim Crow era under the rug, it is important to note that these generations are not too far removed from our current moment in history.

Once we understand the ways in which caste was created and adjusted in order to fit the needs of the dominant caste, we are able to look at America today on a larger scale. Once caste is understood it is much easier to comprehend the current upheaval of our nation. Black people are long tired of trying to fight for true equality in a system that assigns them a script and a label before they are even born into this world. Even the African Americans who are able to rise in class, through athletics, acting, business, or scientific breakthroughs, are still only seen as black people in the eyes of law enforcement and the dominant caste. We are able to see the inequalities that run silently and rampantly through our political, social, and economic systems.

After our eyes have been opened and we are able to see the larger inequalities that persist for the lowest caste in our current day and age, we must then turn our attention inward. We must self-evaluate in order to determine in what ways we have either benefitted or have been harmed by the caste system. We must look to see whether or not we are appropriating the system at large or working, actively, against it. It is important to note that caste continues to exist because of all the people in our country who are silently compliant with it. Caste will not be changed through a law or with the election of a new president but it is imperative that the people who take part in the systems actively work against it. It is no longer enough to be silent and impartial to the caste system that determines so much of a person's life based on traits that they are not able to pick or change.

In all of time there is so much greatness that exists among the most diverse people on the planet. A Puerto Rican composer that is breaking the bounds of creativity, African American doctors that have worked to unearth a cure for Alzheimer's disease or cancer. A young Swedish girl who hopes to leave our planet in a better condition than was left to her. When we continuously assign people to a caste based on their physical traits we miss out on the best and brightest parts of those people. Caste forces people into a predefined box and disallows them to safely exist outside those confines but people were never meant to fit within a predefined role. It is imperative for humanity to see each person as an individual, capable of any dream or path that they set their mind to.

In order to cure the nation of the insidious caste that lurks beneath the surface, we need to start working in more diverse groups. We need to include more marginalized people into places where they are not historically used to being seen like; the CEO's of companies, leadership boards and decision-making teams, equally represented in the media, and accurately portrayed on the news. When we are able to shift our realities to allow people of all cultures, ethnicities, and skin colors the same opportunities and benefits of the dominant caste then the world will be a more expansive and liberated place for all people to exist as they truly desire to and independent of a system who tells them how and what they can be.

It is with compassion and empathy that we bridge the massive artificial gap between human beings. When we are able to identify with one another as fellow humans, as mothers, children, sisters, and law-abiding citizens. When we are able to see one another as working toward individual liberation and freedom of expression rather than give into the fear mongering that pits people against one another than the world is a much better place. And it is with compassion and empathy that we must investigate the past, honor the wrong that has been done historically and actively work to fix and protect the groups that were injured. These steps are imperative for each reader to take in order to bring about positive change as a society. It is through shedding the light onto something that allows it to be tended to and healed. Once we tend to the wounds of our country, we can properly honor the wrong that was done so that history does not repeat itself and does not continue to undermine the efforts of progress today.